Street Marketing™

Street Marketing™

THE FUTURE OF GUERRILLA MARKETING AND BUZZ

Marcel Saucet

Foreword by Derrick Borte

 PRAEGER ™

An Imprint of ABC-CLIO, LLC
Santa Barbara, California • Denver, Colorado

Originally published in French as *Street Marketing™: Un buzz dans la ville!* by Marcel Saucet avec la collaboration de Bernard Cova, copyright © 2013 Les Editions Diateino.

Library of Congress Cataloging-in-Publication Data

Saucet, Marcel.
  Street marketing : the future of guerrilla marketing and buzz / Marcel Saucet.
    pages cm
  Includes bibliographical references.
  ISBN 978-1-4408-3838-5 (hardback) — ISBN 978-1-4408-3839-2 (e-book)
1. Internet marketing. 2. Target marketing. 3. Consumers' preferences.
4. Relationship marketing. I. Title.
  HF5415.1265.S28 2015
  658.8'72—dc23   2015019518

ISBN: 978-1-4408-3838-5
EISBN: 978-1-4408-3839-2

19 18 17 16 15 1 2 3 4 5

This book is also available on the World Wide Web as an eBook.
Visit www.abc-clio.com for details.

Praeger
An Imprint of ABC-CLIO, LLC

ABC-CLIO, LLC
130 Cremona Drive, P.O. Box 1911
Santa Barbara, California 93116-1911

This book is printed on acid-free paper ∞
Manufactured in the United States of America

Contents

New Applications of Street Marketing

Foreword

When I wrote *The Joneses*, a film depicting a make-believe family of stealth marketers, the only exposure I'd had to the use of such guerrilla tactics was an ABC News report years earlier. The groundbreaking and controversial practices included sending a fashion model into bars where she would order a Campari repeatedly in earshot of all the men gravitating around her, or asking a stranger at Disneyland to take a family photo and introducing them to the newest Sony camera. What I was writing seemed to me, and to others who would see the film years later, to be radical notions. I had no idea that I was barely scratching the surface.

As a guest in Dr. Marcel Saucet's class at University of Southern California graduate school to discuss *The Joneses*, I became aware of how much I didn't know. Saucet, a professor of alternative marketing and innovation, contacted me via Twitter and said he was using *The Joneses* as part of the curriculum for his graduate-level classes. I was very interested in meeting him to see how my film fit into his courses, and agreed to visit his class.

That day at USC, Saucet lectured about what is now referred to as "street marketing™," the array of sub-categories which fall under its umbrella, and how this and "stealth" are two dimensions of guerrilla marketing. He presented a powerful overview of what was happening on the cutting edge of marketing, and not only did I become painfully aware of how out of touch I'd been, but I was also hooked by this exciting and rapidly changing subject.

> "Ads are the cave art of the twentieth century."
>
> —*Marshall McLuhan*

It wasn't that long ago that chain-smoking Neanderthal Don Drapers used print, television, and a little basic human psychology to bait the naïve world into doing pretty much anything they wanted. These magicians of Madison Avenue could have a few martinis at lunch, come up with an ad campaign that would hypnotize the world into spending their hard-earned cash, and still have enough time to bang one of the secretaries before heading back to their wives and kids in the post-war suburbia they called home. The simplicity of their power resided not in their ego-fueled machismo, but rather in the fact that everyone on earth got their news and entertainment in one of only a few places, and the ads placed within those media were seen by captive, trusting eyes.

By the turn of the century, the cynicism and distrust of media brought on by the Vietnam War and a host of government and corporate cover-ups, as well as the ever-increasing plurality of media—in the form of five hundred channels and nothing to watch—rendered the old advertising mindset, well . . . old. Around this time, I was in graduate school for Media Studies, and the terms "guerrilla" and "stealth" marketing were beginning to show up. A professor of mine was holding some of the first "online" classes, which, although they were nothing more than a basic group chat session, gave us a peek at the coming democratization of media that was about to rock the world to its core. The concentration of my work became pontificating about how each of us would soon hold in our hands the capacity to create, capture, and distribute news and entertainment on a worldwide scale. And as we've seen throughout the history of media, wherever you find news and entertainment, advertising will not be far behind. After all, it is what pays the bills and buys the content.

This technological explosion that started with the Internet and grew into personal handheld devices has fractured advertising into a level of complexity never seen before. The consumer has become a commodity whose value has grown exponentially along with his or her ability to become a key component of the advertising machine itself.

The year 2015 finds us increasingly aware of the targets placed on our backs by corporations. From the behemoth conglomerates to the latest boutique startups, they are all devoting more and more resources to getting us to buy their products. Advertisers have had to try to stay one step ahead, in the hope of creating top-of-mind awareness and influencing actions that result in sales. New types of advertising are created and identified seemingly daily, such as Ambient, Ambush, Street Marketing™, Viral, Buzz, Undercover, etc.

This book is neither a celebration nor an indictment of today's street marketing practices, but rather an in-depth guide to the history, methods, and trends at the forefront of our complex advertising field, by one of the world's most respected academics on the subject. Saucet illuminates in great detail the most recent innovations, while laying the groundwork for a bigger-picture understanding of where we are going as a consumer culture.

I hope you enjoy it as much as I have.

—Derrick Borte, director and writer
of *The Joneses*, 2010

Introduction

"The street is the umbilical cord that connects the individual to society."

Victor Hugo

The current economic crisis has had a devastating effect on countries worldwide, including many European economies. Despite signs of recovery in Great Britain and the United States, companies still find that they must innovate and keep spending down. The Director of Strategy at a major luxury brand recently told us, for instance, that she did not have enough left in her budget to finance any new advertising campaigns. On the other hand, as soon as we suggested that she take a closer look at street and buzz marketing—because of their high impact and affordability—she was hooked on the idea. This typifies the reaction of many companies today who want to maximize their use of modern communications technologies that succeed in being less expensive but no less effective.

Yet even as companies continue to seek more affordable marketing tools, they still have a daunting number of other market problems to contend with, first and foremost being growing consumer fatigue with conventional communications campaigns. There is just too much advertising, in many people's opinion, with consumers becoming very adept at quickly decoding any and all subliminal messages or affectations. In this somewhat hostile environment, companies have to redesign communications campaigns, in an attempt to increase or maintain market share and/or because they need to lock in existing customers while attracting new ones. Beyond the comfort of traditional platforms like television, radio, cinema, and press—media whose relationship with customers involves a certain remoteness—and irrespective of their sector of activity, companies are more than ready today to hit the streets and invent new communication methods.

Alongside this, the explosion in ICT (new information and communications technologies, led by the Internet and social media) offers a whole range of new communications tools. These can actually be quite ambivalent, however, reflecting consumers' growing role as prescribers who are more sheltered than ever before (because of all the help they receive from specialist organizations), but also reflecting consumers' growing willingness to use a variety of tools to share their experiences and feelings. Meeting as communities, disseminating information en masse, are new actors representing an opportunity but also a threat for companies. The business world is forced to adapt and has started to focus on developing its online presence, using the Internet to create a relationship with consumers that is more complete, more direct, and above all quicker than in the past.

Against this backdrop, companies have understood that it is only through a general questioning of their modes of communication that they will have any chance of remaining attractive. Hence the advent of unconventional communications approaches, spearheaded by street marketing. This translates to the rise of communications operations established outside of conventional points-of-sales, and more specifically in the street, where direct contacts with consumers can be entertained. The approach encompasses a whole range of techniques intended to invigorate street life and touch customers as they go about their daily lives. It ranges from simple product tests to happenings or flash mobs that are akin to street theater.

The main purpose of this book is to initiate marketing and/or communications practitioners and students into something that is progressively turning into the marketing of the future. Through numerous current examples, it describes the changes that have caused marketing to nurture these new communications approaches, starting with street marketing and the buzz associated with it. Once readers have finished this book and gained a full understanding of the different approaches it enumerates, they will view street marketing (and the word-of-mouth that it generates) as a real opportunity for any manager seeking to increase the public's familiarity with his or her company, while promoting its products or services directly to customers who have become increasingly demanding and difficult to satisfy.

The first section describes the full range of unconventional marketing techniques (viral, stealth, ambush, etc.). The second concentrates on the emergence of a street culture within which a number of specific codes have arisen, codes that brands are broadly replicating in their communications. The third shows readers the organization of street marketing campaigns, which are invariably disseminated via a buzz marketing approach. The fourth and final section offers a panorama of the areas where such techniques might be applied. Three key ideas are developed in relation to unconventional marketing techniques, specifically involving street and buzz marketing:

- They constitute a direct response to social change
- They are clearly turning into the marketing of the future
- They are a great opportunity for most companies

Thanks to this book, readers will be able to identify obstacles impeding conventional communications campaigns in today's world. The message here is that the most appropriate responses to these problems might in fact be new marketing concepts. What the book ultimately reveals are the key factors in a successful street marketing campaign. What it does not try to do is offer a purely negative critique of conventional communications campaigns. Instead, it attempts to flesh out the panoply of techniques that a communications or marketing specialist might use. In other words, the focus here is intentionally placed on operational issues. The purpose of this practical orientation is to highlight which traps should be avoided and what are the best practices to implement. Toward this end, the book uses a great many examples (several dozen companies were consulted in total) and combines them with interviews of 180 street marketing professionals.[1] In addition (and to make it more fun to read), the book proposes a whole range of practical tools—meaning that all throughout there are definitions initiating readers into the specific language used in unconventional marketing approaches. Lastly, the book's numerous references give readers with particular interests a chance to continue discovering the captivating world of street marketing.

Marketing Today

Chapter 1

The Crisis in Conventional Marketing

Alternative marketing is a direct response to both consumers' changing expectations and social change. But like any unconventional approach, it also constitutes a necessity for brands.

Operations of this kind have two main advantages. First, their operationalization and development costs are generally much lower than traditional media-based campaigns. Also, because they are so original, they also give brands an opportunity to generate a great deal of buzz about their communications strategies.

The economic problems that the world faces today have forced companies to be particularly creative in terms of figuring out how to retain consumers' affections.[1] Above and beyond the fact that modern consumers are less inclined to consume without thinking about what they are doing, they also tend to possess greater product expertise and more detailed knowledge of the different attributes of a given product. In part, this explains why consumers are less reluctant nowadays to abandon one brand's products for another that better satisfies their expectations.

Along with this, companies also have to contend with an increase in multi-competition, something that has become a real problem for many businesses. In their efforts to increase market share, they have to adapt to all these new handicaps even as they try to grow sales.

A communications campaign always pursues one of two goals: enhanced consumer recognition or promoting a product, service, or brand. Unconventional marketing campaigns can offer a response to some of the contextual constraints discussed above.

First, the new operations—either because they are digital and/or because they take place outside of points of sales—help brands to create more direct contact with consumers, who tend to expect greater transparency from companies today.

Second, such campaigns can generate significant returns on investment if the company is able to generate a major buzz. This is because they generally cost less than traditional campaigns. But if successful, they can be just as effective.

Third, these operations are not only financially optimal but also improve a company's brand image. Originality is something that companies can use to show consumers that they are willing to surprise them and work with them as equals, even as they emphasize their sense of innovation and creativity. Consumers quickly become aware of—and grateful for—the efforts that the company is making.

In short, these kinds of unconventional methods seem opportune and even necessary for brands that find it harder and harder to ensure existing customers' loyalty while (and above all) attracting new ones. This is not to say that the new approaches offer an immediate solution to today's economic crisis. They are, however, original and effective ways of responding to the main constraints that business faces at present.

In the wake of brands such as the Mini, Coca-Cola, Red Bull, or Ben & Jerry's, many companies now grasp the usefulness of these campaigns, incorporating into their budgets a number of development cost items specific to new communications techniques. A prime example is the impactful interactive digital campaign waged by Tipp-Ex,[2] a best-selling European brand of correction fluid and related correction products, similar to Wite-Out in the United States. The Tipp-Ex(perience) series of videos feature a bear and a hunter. In one, the hunter asks the viewer to choose whether or not he should shoot the bear. If the viewer selects "shoot the bear," the hunter refuses. The hunter then takes a Tipp-Ex and deletes the word "shoot"; the viewer then has the opportunity to write in any verb to replace "shoot." If he writes "dance," the viewer will see a video of the hunter dancing with the bear. Tipp-Ex produced forty different video scenarios for forty verb choices. In another campaign, the hunter and the bear are having a birthday party. An incoming missile threatens to disrupt the party, and the viewer selects "end the party" or "don't end the party." This was among the most buzz-worthy video campaigns of 2011, generating more than 20 million hits on YouTube in less than two years.

THE NEED FOR UNCONVENTIONAL APPROACHES

More than an opportunity, the use of unconventional marketing has become a necessity for brands. Given the many different kinds of marketing that have been invented since 1984, it is very hard to identify with any precision what constitutes an unconventional approach. A general overview in Table 1.1 gives an idea of the wide range of new marketing categories that have been invented in recent years.

In 1984, Jay Conrad Levinson mentioned the concept of guerrilla marketing for the first time. He saw this as an alternative and unconventional type of marketing, one whose main advantage was its cost. In his

Table 1.1 Marketing Concepts, 1984–2014

• Anti-Marketing	• Geo-Marketing	• Reverse Marketing
• Authenticity Marketing	• Grass Roots Marketing	• Societal Marketing
• Buzz Marketing	• Green Marketing	• Solution Marketing
• Cause-Related Marketing	• Guerrilla Marketing	• Stakeholder Marketing
• Celebrity Marketing	• Holistic Marketing	• Stealth Marketing
• Chronomarketing	• Interactive Marketing	• Street Marketing
• Co-Marketing	• Knowledge Marketing	• Sustainable Marketing
• Community Marketing	• Life Event Marketing	• Symbiotic Marketing
• Contextual Marketing	• Macro-Marketing	• Scarcity Marketing
• Convergence Marketing	• Maxi Marketing	• Sensory Marketing
• Counter Marketing	• Mega Marketing	• Situational Marketing
• Customer Centric Marketing	• Micro-Marketing	• Slow Marketing
• Database Marketing	• Multilevel Marketing	• Social Marketing
• Eco-Marketing	• Multisensory Marketing	• Time-Based Marketing
• Emotion Marketing	• Network Marketing	• Total Relationship
• Empowerment Marketing	• Niche Marketing	• Trade Marketing
• Environmental Marketing	• Non-Business Marketing	• Trend Marketing
• Ethnic Marketing	• Nostalgia Marketing	• Tribal Marketing

(Continued)

Table 1.1 (*Continued*)

• Ethno-Marketing	• Olfactory Marketing	• Turbo Marketing
• Entrepreneurial Marketing	• One-to-One Marketing	• Undercover Marketing
• Event Marketing	• Permission Marketing	• Value Marketing
• Expeditionary Marketing	• Radical Marketing	• Viral Marketing
• Experience Marketing	• Real-Time Marketing	• Yield Marketing
• Exponential Marketing	• Relationship Marketing	
• Family Marketing	• Retro-Marketing	

Source: Bernard Cova, Gregorio Fuschillo, and Marcel Saucet (2014), "Attualità e prospettive dello Street Marketing," *Micro & Macro Marketing*, 1, 145–166.

thinking, guerrilla marketing is for people who have ambitious dreams for their activity but not much money.[3] This meant that unconventional (alternative) marketing exists, by definition, in opposition to commercial marketing, which became a fully fledged discipline in 1960, notably with McCarthy's launch of the 4 P's,[4] representing "all actions whose purpose is to predict and observe—and where necessary, stimulate, revive or renew—consumers' need for a particular category of products or services, while adapting the productive and commercial apparatus of a company to the needs determined in this way."

The recent rise of concepts such as brand image, umbrella brand, or family brand seems to have caused many companies to start questioning their own marketing approaches. Even the very top brands are starting to engage in guerrilla marketing, deviating from previous trajectories and focusing on small-budget actions, to such an extent that this has become an integral part of their marketing strategy. Companies like Nike or Ikea no longer have any compunction about resorting regularly to this new kind of marketing.

The question then becomes whether conventional marketing is in crisis; whether the rise of alternative marketing might be construed as a simple reshuffling of the deck; and whether the two types of marketing complement one another.

Unlike so-called conventional marketing, alternative (or nonconformist) marketing is difficult to define. For one thing, it is difficult to ascertain which particular properties or characteristics should be associated with it. Depending on which definitions are used, it might also be deemed to cover so-called modern communications techniques that are not expected to last very long yet still feature as temporary solutions (albeit with limited validity). It is difficult to say for sure at a time when otherwise exceptional techniques are fast becoming the norm.

One frequent comparison is between conventional and digital (or viral) marketing. When this latter variant first developed, it was often presented as a kind of fashion. Today, however, digital marketing constitutes an integral part of all conventional or unconventional communications strategies. The idea that opposition remains at this level is no longer considered valid. A better way to discuss this is by highlighting the proliferation of different marketing platforms and questioning their complementarity.

Today's consumers want to be won back, almost as if the big brands had been unfaithful to them. They also expect to be surprised. This active re-conquest must be innovative and demonstrate the usefulness of guerrilla marketing. It must satisfy demands for a quick return on investment; the need to produce a variety of actions that consumers find attractive; and the need to surprise people. The end result is that brands today are increasingly organizing lightning-quick operations that they hope will allow them to make their mark and attract widespread attention.

As an ancillary aspect, some brands have in recent years seemed quite hypocritical and cut off from reality.[5] And even those that gear their marketing strategies towards consumers' centers of interest often forget how negatively people can react to very expensive communications campaigns (like commercials showing gas-guzzling SUVs at a time of high fuel prices).

These conditions increase the attractiveness of guerrilla marketing as something that is physically and ideologically closer to consumers. It is often said that marketing must satisfy consumers' needs. This is difficult, however, when the real objective of any marketing strategy is to create need and provoke desire in a way that is unexpected, innovative, and surprising.

The notion of perceived value is also crucial to strategic understanding at this level. Brand value can no longer be solely measured, in (brand) image terms, using traditional marketing mix logic. Instead, the focus today is on a brand's actions and attitudes. Guerrilla marketing can be used to personify a brand. There is nothing better for brand than to go out into the street and campaign, in much the same way that the popular politicians of yesteryear used to do.

THE EMERGENCE OF UNCONVENTIONAL MARKETING

The Economic Crisis and Its Implications for Communication Budgets

The 2008 crisis affected many economic actors worldwide, hitting communications budgets for large brands (but also, and even more so, for smaller ones). According to national surveys published in 2014 by emarketer.com,[6] in Q1 2012 the world's top media platforms suffered a sharp drop in year-to-year advertising revenues (−4.2% for television, −8.1% for the press). Having said that, companies' analysis of their shrinking television budgets had progressively taught them to budget differently during times of crisis, so that they now either used more expensive commercials more creatively, or else simply settled for less expensive ones. Additionally, figures for two other leading media platforms, cinema and online, recorded rising advertising revenues during the same period, up respectively by 10.1 percent and 5.5 percent. All in all, however, there has been a major downturn in advertising revenues since 2011. Forced to cut budgets while maintaining their performance targets, companies have had to approach the issue of communications from an entirely new angle, changing their attitudes about how advertising campaigns should be created and disseminated.

Along with this financial challenge, companies have had to figure out how to communicate with consumers—who are becoming increasingly turned off by the growing number of commercials they see every day—in a way that is both innovative and untraditional.

Consumers' Saturation by Commercial Messages and the Emergence of New Advertising Campaigns

In his book *Propagandes silencieuses* [Silent propaganda], Ignacio Ramonet[7] asserted that consumers are exposed to something like two hundred commercial messages every day. This advertising saturation makes it necessary for brands to communicate more effectively while innovating continuously. To keep product sales up, companies must find new ways of influencing their target consumers and get them to buy. Sponsors and communications agencies must also find new platforms to keep audiences' attention up.

Traditional approaches to brand promotion and communication have included:

- Ambient advertising, which permeates public places (store floors, park benches, gas stations, etc.). This has become increasingly widespread due to the constant increase in products' purchasing costs and also because of competition;

- Product placement, which consist of presenting a brand's products in a way that uses memorization effects to influence consumers; and
- Digital advertising, which has become increasingly important in consumers' daily lives.

These different means of communication have been widely tried and tested over the years. Yet they seem to be running out of steam today, due to the growing fatigue of consumers who have been overly exposed to conventional advertising messages, the omnipresence and intrusive nature of which makes them ineffective.

This dynamic has given birth to street marketing (and guerrilla marketing, from which it is derived)—not forgetting buzz marketing, generational marketing, and wait marketing.

These new forms of marketing have not only heightened consumers' curiosity and sparked media resonance but are also affordable. Distributing Nike leaflets to senior citizens, while dressed in Nike colors, or building a temporary tennis court to host a match between two players in a New York City street—none of this requires much preparation time or effort. The same applies to the idea of leaving stacks of advertising leaflets in coffee shops and other public places, spending a mere $1,120 for 10,000 leaflets that are likely to last much longer than a campaign would. It is worth remembering that consumers themselves have also evolved over time to develop greater expertise, making it harder to influence them using brand-driven consumption incentives. Advertising today must stand out because it is original but also because it uses new technologies and media while incorporating a new sense of consumer-oriented playfulness—all in a bid to convert consumers from spectators to engaged actors.

Some brands no longer hesitate to use consumers' downtime (for instance, when people are travelling) to shower them with advertising. One example was *Spiderman 2*'s promotional campaign showing a urinal built at the top of a wall, illustrating the film brand's desire to attract consumers' attention as they went about their daily business.

Sprite demonstrated this successfully in 2012, when it created several giant showers on a sandy beach in Brazil, representing branded drink dispensers, accompanied by the slogan "Refresh Your Ideas." This innovative and unusual campaign was fun for consumers, with 1,500 bottles being distributed daily. It strengthened people's memorization of the brand and enhanced its visibility.

Another form of communication is outdoor marketing, as Hayari demonstrated so successfully in 2013 at Paris and New York on *Vogue*

Photo 1.1   The Hayari street marketing operation in Paris, France. (Used by permission)

fashion night. They built a carriage for a newly married bride, wearing a Hayari bridal gown and perfume. As the carriage drove along the street during fashion night, perfume samples were given to people who congratulated the bride, eventually attracting more people. The operation managed to create buzz on the street and get the audience to come toward the brand rather than the brand trying to acquire its audience. This strengthened brand visibility and memorability. Photo 1.1 shows people with their perfume samples, the carriage, and the bride.

With a new concept called "skinvertisement," the consumers themselves become promotional tools, accepting payment in exchange for having a brand's logo tattooed on visible parts of their bodies. This phenomenon attests to advertising's ubiquity in people's lives, while also illustrating brands' inventiveness in optimizing representations and creating a buzz.

Another concept that has also appeared in the world of brand communications is "flogos," involving the use of fun new ecological communications platforms. Widespread in the United States, these flying logos can be made out of items including wire, soap, helium, or compressed air. They tend to be molded in a template before being floated like balloons for around forty minutes, after which they disappear without leaving a trace. Flogos constitute a new, innovative, and inexpensive way of promoting products through communications platforms.

Advertising affects consumption, notably where young people between the ages of fifteen and twenty are concerned. Studies demonstrate that this group's mode of consumption partially depends on circles of close friends but also on what they see in the street, attesting to advertising's impact if done effectively and innovatively.

Irrespective of consumers' age, however, brands have been entering a number of new fields in an attempt to satisfy customer needs. Haribo, for instance, customized an entire escalator in Germany to promote its famous wild licorice candy. Organized by an agency called ServicePlan, the event constituted a new kind of fun communication, one that provoked consumers' curiosity while facilitating brand memorization.

Another example is PizzaHacker in the United States, which wanted to be number one in the listings for organic pizza in San Francisco. PizzaHacker is the brick-and-mortar incarnation of a pop-up venture that went with a wild concept of selling organic pizzas on the streets with ovens on wheels. Communication was conducted solely through Twitter and inspired by guerrilla marketing.

Also worth a look is the communications campaign promoting the 2007 season of *Dexter*, a TV series broadcast on Showtime Network. An agency called Pop2Life was responsible for this event, which centered around public fountains in fourteen American cities. Each fountain was wrapped in crime scene tape, reinforcing the campaign's overall theme. The water itself was dyed red to look like blood—the series'

Photo 1.2   The PizzaHacker street marketing operation. (Used by permission)

famous "brand image." Teams dressed in white coats with the series' name on their backs went around distributing flyers to bystanders to tell them about the new season. Running these actions at the same time in several large cities helped the campaign to generate a major buzz almost immediately.

Another example of a campaign promoting a TV program was for the second season of *The Sopranos*, a New York Mafia show broadcast on HBO. Aside from its intriguing aspects (epitomized, for instance, by having artificial arms placed to extend from the trunks of New York City taxis), unlike *Dexter*, this campaign was only run in New York City itself. As such, it constituted an example of geo-marketing, where the physical location of an action becomes its center of focus.

Along similar lines, it is worth noting a similar example of limbs extending from vehicles, namely arms hung from buses to promote a new horror video game called *Resident Evil*.[8]

The squeeze on budgets has also translated into some advertising campaigns using the Internet as the main communications channel for recycling things they have done before. One example was Budweiser's year 2000 viral commercial, transformed in 2008 into an ad supporting Barack Obama.

Elsewhere, a campaign promoting the iPod Nano allowed people to add their own banners to an existing billboard, to communicate their personal activities. This was an ambush marketing operation run by the Canadian agency Bos. The idea was to take advantage of other companies' advertising actions and redirect them in a way that stood out from the crowd.

Brands use a multitude of different communications platforms, as witnessed by the advertising that Fiat did in Germany for its Ducato utility vehicle. In this instance, the automobile's rear doors opened to reveal a parking space generally reserved for shopping carts. The idea was to promote the car's spacious trunk, which was big enough to fit three rows of carts.

Then there was McDonalds' Free Coffee Operation, where an agency called Cossette transformed a lamppost into a coffee pot pouring into a McDonald's cup, bearing the slogan "Free coffee is ready." The agency also came up with the idea of three-dimensional bus shelter ads offering coffee. A plume of steam made the illusion seem unbelievably real.

Then there was a campaign in collaboration with Cartier, Chopard, Piaget, and Vendome jewelry store in Juan-les-Pins, on the French Riviera, to promote special discounts for winter. They created a "luxury squad" street marketing campaign, in which a police-like brigade located near the store halted passers-by who were wearing jewels in bad taste and issued them "fine" tickets for 20 percent to 50 percent discounts. This operation reached three hundred people in one day.

Movie theaters have also been adopting new and more impactful way of communicating, epitomized by the promotion of the second season of the American program *The Walking Dead*. Here, just as spectators at a theater in Sandton, South Africa, were getting ready to watch the trailer of a romantic comedy, a zombie entered the room and started stumbling over people, startling and frightening them. The end came when the heroine of the on-screen trailer shot the zombie, saving the spectators. This interaction with spectators showed how it is possible to promote an event effectively yet inexpensively by using consumers to create a buzz.

A LEADER IN ALTERNATIVE MARKETING: STREETANDMARKETING.COM

There is no doubt that alternative marketing approaches creating original and creative brand images (and enhancing brands' visibility) have become increasingly widespread. They do, however, require specific competencies, not only in terms of strategic marketing but also (and above all) with regards to their operational aspects. This is because alternative marketing does not consist only of finding a good idea and implementing it. It also necessitates a deep analysis of the target selected even before the operation commences—not to mention major organizational capabilities.

This explains the rise of a number of communications agencies in the United States and Europe specializing in these new communications techniques: streetandmarketing.com, Saatchi & Saatchi, Alt Terrain, ubi bene, Torke, JWT, Tm Advertising, Hot Cow, Attack Marketing, I am beyond, Curb, Icimars, Anolis, C*RED, Le Village, Vanksen, Cossette, Streetjam, Tesko, You to You, Milk and Mint, Mission, Pearltrees, Fearless, Cunnings, etc. The mission of these agencies is to find campaign ideas that fit the sponsor company's values and also its customers' expectations.

Among all these agencies, one has developed a reputation as being the most effective in terms of market presence: LCA Street Marketing (www.streetandmarketing.com).

Streetandmarketing.com[9] is known for the originality of its campaigns and for the advice it offers brands including Deezer, Universal, Azzaro, Feelunique.com, Thierry Mugler, Swarovsky, Merck, Porsche Design, DRESR, Taryn Rose shoes, Fig and Olives, the United Nations, Lanvin, Intel, Sony, and Microsoft. The agency, which specializes in discovering future street marketing trends, enjoyed a 25 percent increase in revenue thanks to its brand Street Marketing™, which focuses on street communications, including alternative billboards, distribution of flyers, or simply new kinds of flash mobs. Concepts are created in streetandmarketing.com laboratories located in France and the United States, where they are tested before being rolled out. Drawing on research from a number of North American sources (all employees are either doctors, psychoanalysts, professors, or PhDs), the laboratory works with companies willing to question themselves, innovate, and go into the streets. Customers also receive consultancy training to open employees' minds to the importance of brand. Campaign ROI studies are directly connected to street marketing research undertaken by agency representatives who worked in American universities before publishing in a number of academic journals including the *Harvard Business Review, Journal of Marketing Communications, Decisions Marketing*, and *Journal of Micro and Macro Marketing*.

One example of this work is the sexy car wash campaign that the agency created for Hertz in the Caribbean. The agency also offered to create an innovative but inexpensive guerrilla marketing campaign communicating to Jack Daniels' male target group the friendship values associated with drinking this Tennessee whisky. Possibilities at this level are unlimited. Indeed, before moving on to the featured Jack Daniels advertisement, it might be worthwhile for readers to consider what ideas they might like to have proposed.

Chapter 2

Unconventional Marketing

Among all the approaches that have arisen, alternative marketing—known to many as viral marketing—with its reliance on social media, tends to be the most popular.[1] Managers' favorite approach, on the other hand, tends to be street marketing.[2]

Unlike viral marketing, street marketing has yet to be fully conceptualized, and there is no clear idea about what actions it covers. Nor is it fully understood what this category has in common with other forms of unconventional marketing, or even its differences with them (not to mention its advantages and drawbacks, which have yet to be specified). The purpose of this chapter is therefore to help managers to decide why, how, and when to use unconventional marketing approaches and street marketing, by illustrating what each variant represents. It starts with a case study involving Heineken, to build a typology covering the full range of unconventional marketing approaches.

CASE STUDY: HEINEKEN

In 2010, Heineken used the Champions League (specifically, a match between Real Madrid and AC Milan) to launch a new unconventional marketing operation aimed at generating as much buzz as possible. Consumers were not aware that the event was part of an entire communications campaign. More than a hundred women convinced their boyfriends (all AC Milan fans) to attend a classical music and poetry event, instead of watching the Champions League final. Fifty professors also got their students to attend the concert instead of watching the match, with a number of journalists also being sent there by their bosses. In most cases, participants were joined by their girlfriends (who pretended that their fathers had recommended the place and loved the concert). All in all, nearly two hundred persons were brought in by the brand. The aim was to trick more than a thousand AC Milan fans into finding themselves in the same place.

For the event, Heineken had rented a concert hall large enough to host the thousands who attended. When the curtain was lifted, it revealed a "hypnotic" music orchestra, plus a giant screen showing different messages. After fifteen minutes, Heineken's operation started to reach a crescendo, with the orchestra playing the Champions League theme and showing messages like "It is hard saying no to the boss" on the screen. Having lured them to the event under false pretenses, a final message cleared things up for the fans: "Did you believe for one second that we would have you miss the match?" People started applauding when "Enjoy the match with Heineken" was flashed, and the game was then shown in full. The audience was over the moon, experiencing an authentic moment of enjoyment that had been visually dominated by the Heineken logo.

The operation had an enormous impact. More than 1,136 spectators were in the concert hall, with 1.5 million people watching the match live on Skyport, and more than 10 million hearing about the operation in local media. In less than two weeks, 5 million people had heard about the operation online, with many praising it on blogs, forums, and social media. The video was a great success on YouTube, which counted 562,000 hits. On BlogBang it was viewed more than 243,459 times. On social media—which constitutes a bona fide measurement tool nowadays—the event was seen by more than 6.2 million persons who liked Heineken, with more than 99,983 leaving comments. Browsing Google for "Heineken: Guerrilla Marketing Event in Italy" produces more than 52,500 results. "Heineken Italy Activation Milan AC Real Madrid" has more than 35,200.

FOUR TYPES OF UNCONVENTIONAL MARKETING

Today a whole set of communications and marketing approaches call themselves "unconventional," claiming to be alternatives to traditional Kotlerian marketing management approaches.[3] Within this perpetually growing jungle of new terms, "guerrilla marketing"—introduced in 1984 by Jay Conrad Levinson—constitutes an umbrella term[4] referring to any (very) affordable unconventional communications system involving imaginativeness and sometimes operating at the borders of ethical behavior. Guerrilla marketing has revived a whole array of pre-Kotlerian methods of communication, including word-of-mouth, walking advertisements (such as sandwich board carriers), and subliminal advertising.

A deeper look at this jungle of unconventional approaches reveals a profusion of terms such as ambient, ambush, buzz, stealth, street, undercover, and viral—all attesting to the boundless creativity of marketing specialists. Academic literature has done very little at this level, however, and there is a dearth of seminal unconventional marketing texts, or articles in specialist marketing scientific reviews highlighting the specifics of one of the other alternative approach. Only by looking at more generalist management reviews such as *Business Horizons*[5] or *California Management Review*[6] does it become possible to find scientific articles on the new approaches.

According to the literature, one point that all of these alternative approaches do have in common is the promise of communications results that are equal if not superior to conventional approaches—but at less cost. This resonates with the definition of viral marketing given by Levinson in his seminal text,[7] where this variant is depicted as something that allows companies to promote their products and services with very small budgets while maintaining the same level of sensitivity as achieved through television advertising.[8] Note as well Levinson's view of stealth marketing as a particularly viable alternative to traditional advertising—largely because consumers perceive it as a more flexible and personal kind of communication.[9] Of course, none of these approaches is independent from the others: viral marketing is a neighbor of stealth marketing and the equivalent of buzz marketing; ambient marketing encompasses street marketing and mobilizes viral marketing[10]; stealth marketing or undercover marketing uses viral marketing as one of its main techniques and ambush marketing[11] as one of its main application contexts; and ambush or parasitic marketing does the same with viral marketing.[12]

In short, unconventional (or alternative) marketing—which some people call guerrilla marketing—has given birth to four main interdependent approaches. In turn, they encompass other neighboring approaches (with ambient marketing being the closest to street marketing).

Viral Marketing

Derived from word-of-mouth and the influence this has on consumers, according to Katz and Lazarsfeld (1955), viral marketing constitutes an electronic word-of-mouth, where a marketing message relating to a

Table 2.1   Advantages and Drawbacks of Viral Marketing

Advantages	Drawbacks
• Greater creative license afforded due to the message delivery medium being more intimate and customized.	• Viral marketing quickly becomes diluted through misinterpretation.
• The viral process increases the speed with which the message is disseminated and maintains its integrity.	• Viral marketing has become a jargonistic buzzword that people do not understand very well.
• The message can be more targeted, increasing the likelihood of it actually reaching interested individuals.	• It takes a long time and a great deal of up-front investment to create the kind of buzz that spreads on its own.
• The receiver of a viral message is more likely to be amenable to it because the sender has implicitly endorsed the message by passing it on.	• Putting out a message and having it go viral can be as much a liability as an asset.
• There is synergistic value in integrating online and offline marketing strategies.	

company, brand, or product is transmitted at an exponentially increasing rate, most of the time using social media.[13] Creating "buzz" (a.k.a. viral marketing) is therefore an operation that requires almost no budget and has the potential to take place before, during, and after a product launch or event. It can also be disseminated very rapidly and on a grand scale to a very large number of persons. (See Table 2.1.)

One example was the buzz about the smartphone battle between Blackberry and Apple. Blackberry started this viral war with an online commercial that was a frontal attack on its main competitor, showing a blackberry piercing an apple like bullet fired from a gun.[14] Apple[15] responded right away with an online commercial showing a blackberry being squashed by an impenetrable apple, featuring the two-word strap line "Simple facts." The suggestion here was that apples have never been crushed by blackberries, symbolizing the technical and/or technological superiority of the one company over the other.

Stealth Marketing

Already considered part of subliminal advertising, Vince Packard's seminal text from 1957, *Hidden Persuaders*, described stealth marketing as a deliberate action to enter, play, or exit the market secretly and without being seen, or at least an attempt to do so.[16] Other terms used for this approach have included "undercover marketing" and "covert marketing." One recent example[17] was an operation in New York City where a female model asked passersby to take a picture of her, pretending she wanted a holiday souvenir. The idea was that they would then have to handle her phone, a brand new Blackberry product.

Stealth marketing is a more subtle and less aggressive practice than its predecessors. As theorized by Roy and Chattopadhyay in 2010, it consists of tricking consumers by advertising a brand surreptitiously. Beyoncé recently organized a clever stealth marketing operation by filming a fake fight between her sister and husband Jay Z in an elevator. After the press broadcast this video, sales of her latest album rose by 200 percent, without purchasers being aware that they were part of a communications operation. In 2009 Hollywood did a movie about this called *The Joneses*, directed by Derrick Borte. The story involved a fake family of consumers who were actually marketing professionals paid to get their new neighbors to buy into the image of a perfect family in order to sell them a whole range of products.[18]

To promote the movie *Limitless*, an entire stealth marketing campaign was planned using a video where a man filmed himself in Times Square showing people a gadget that he had invented, which would enable him to pirate screens worldwide simply by inserting a chip and then linking this to his telephone so he could forward whatever image was being filmed.[19] At the end, the man told everyone he had gotten this ingenious idea after taking a pill that allowed him to use the full capacity of his mind. People went crazy online looking for the drug, with websites created for the occasion linking back to the movie. The trailer experienced the same kind of enthusiasm, counting so far more than 3,659,094 views online.

Another original example of stealth marketing was Gillette's use of action film star Jean-Claude Van Damme. Known for his temper and odd way of speaking, Van Damme agreed to become a focus of mockery. In a video made à la *Candid Camera*, Van Damme could be seen getting angry at a cameraman filming a commercial for Gillette, with the director desperately trying to remake the sequence into a scene from Swan Lake.[20] The question here is whether the actor was really upset or if this was part of the commercial. The video was viewed more than a million times online.

Comparing the colossal sums spent by brands for advertisements meant to be broadcast via traditional media, as opposed to the infinitely smaller sums associated with guerrilla marketing operations—and given the minimal difference in both marketing strategies' potential—it is easy to understand why leading U.S. companies are starting to use stealth marketing, with the wave also reaching European shores now. (See Table 2.2.)

Table 2.2   Advantages and Drawbacks of Stealth Marketing

Advantages	Drawbacks
• Creates a confort zone • Reaches potential customers who tend otherwise to mistrust advertising • Generates a grassroots buzz capable of going viral • Gives customers a sense of "discovering" a valuable product or service • Less of a financial investment	• Campaign aspect cannot be masked • Consumers may sense that they have been manipulated • Many see undercover marketing as being unethical • Nicknamed "roach baiting" by critics • Seen as a method for manipulating consumers dishonestly

Ambush Marketing

Originating during the 1984 Los Angeles Olympic Games, when companies who had not received IOC authorization tried to launch communications operations piggybacking the event's huge profile, ambush marketing—also known as "parasitic marketing"—has been defined as a form of co-marketing that organizations use to gain recognition, attention, or any other benefit from being associated with an event or product with which they no direct or official connection.[21] One 2007 example was when the Dim lingerie company used a rugby match between France and Ireland to show pretty young women wearing the brand's products. This attracted the cameras of French TV station TF1, which showed the women cheering. Using a tiny budget, Dim was able to communicate with something like 14 million TV spectators. It took no time at all for the buzz to build up, and despite a few tensions with the International Rugby Board (IRB), the operation was a great success for Dim.[22]

The principle of ambush (or parasitic) marketing is to use the mediatization of a sporting, political, private, musical, and other events for one's own advertising purposes, via platforms such as T-shirts or posters. Along with this, ambush marketing can also involve street actions, such as using posters meant for a particular purpose to serve another.

Sports or private events (or gala evenings) are not the only way of staging an ambush marketing campaign. In 2010 at one of Barack Obama's open meetings,[23] three men wearing Abercrombie & Fitch (a trendy brand for 18- to 25-year-olds) stood up behind the president. This gave the brand great exposure and visibility while costing nothing.

Another ambush operation was during the 2011 Rugby World Cup in New Zealand. The English international Manu Tuilagi broke official sponsorship rules by wearing an Opro mouthguard featuring the brand's logo. The idea was to use World Cup media coverage (and the

Table 2.3   Advantages and Drawbacks of Ambush Marketing

Advantages	Drawbacks
• Benefits from popularity of a well-known stage or event without having to make the typically significant financial contribution that is usually required on such occasions • Considerably less expensive than other options, which involve paying fees to official sponsors • Considerably improves notoriety of brand/company/NGO while allowing it to acquire and capitalize on event's values (e.g., on sporting values) • Technique has been wildly successful for marketing specialists who have used it in the past • Short-lived nature makes it difficult for event organizers curtail the marketing operation through legal proceedings	• Despite excellence, such campaigns are often at the limit of legality and regularly provoke legal responses • Ambush marketing specialists cannot use words, logos, or images from the official event • Requires good legal knowledge and ability to come up with exceptionally creative solutions • Controversial aspect may also taint company's good image

player's own fame) to display a product that had not been approved by the official event sponsors. Opro denied having anything to do with this (illegal) ambush marketing, and the International Federation of Rugby fined the player.[24] Clearly, however, the event's mediatization raised the brand's profile. (See Table 2.3.)

A further example was when McDonald's used the Chicago St. Patrick's Day parade, during which the Chicago River is dyed green, to publicize its Shamrock Shake. An enormous empty McDonald's milkshake cup lying on the ground on its side gave the impression that its green contents had spilled into the river. McDonald's benefited from enormous (free) visibility due to this action, which was covered by local TV station CLTV. Proceeds from sales of the green drinks were given to the Ronald McDonald House foundation.[25]

McDonald's also used the St. Patrick's Day parade for a second ambush marketing operation, running a float that resembled Ronald McDonald's shoe. The idea was to give their clown a vantage point he could use to wave to the crowd.

Ambient Marketing

This particular marketing variant originated in the United States with the old sandwich men who used to carry advertising boards through city streets. In France, it originated with the walls of buildings dotting the nation's road network being painted in the colors of Dubonnet (an alcoholic drink). Some observers have defined ambient marketing as a complex form of corporate communication mobilizing elements taken from the external environment and potentially using any type of physical surface to transmit messages capable of generating consumer commitment.[26] Ambient and street marketing are close but differ in certain respects, as discussed below.

Hubba Bubba chewing gum used an ambient strategy in 2009 to praise its product's main characteristics. Saying it sold the world's longest chewing gum, the brand completely covered a billboard with gum, showing everyone just how big the stick really was.[27]

Because ambient marketing is based on an interactive practice (one often driven by the consumers themselves), it differs greatly from "passive" TV advertising by helping to root the product advertisement in a real context. Categorizing an operation as involving street or ambient marketing requires that it be directly connected to the street. Otherwise it should be called outdoor marketing, which includes, for instance, all of the different operations that might take place in train stations or public spaces without having any direct links to the outside world.

A good example was the store launch of Sony's new PSP console, when the company customized the central court of an international tennis tournament to make it look like a gigantic games console. Similarly, September 9, 2009, saw a famous ambient operation marking the DVD launch of the cult horror film *Chucky*, which had been made twenty years before. An army of terrifying dolls invaded New York's Times Square, frightening everyone who came across them.[28]

La Française des Jeux lottery organization collaborated with the BETC agency to build in Paris's Opera district a wooden billboard equipped with a digital sensor showing how many people actually touched the object. Its slogan was "Touch wood, you might get lucky." The operation coincided with the Friday, January 13, 2012, Super Loto draw.[29] The campaign cost almost nothing but got people talking about La Française des Jeux.

Academic research tends to recognize four leading unconventional marketing approaches. However, one of the aforementioned studies (SDA, from spring 2011) opines that marketing managers seem to be primarily focused on viral and ambient marketing, ignoring the stealth and ambush variants because they are considered less ethical. The idea being put forward here was that managers essentially view unconventional marketing as a viral communications approach based on word-of-mouth and facilitated by the advent of social media, and/or that

Photo 2.1   An ambient marketing operation run by Kit Kat, a Nestlé group brand. (Courtesy of Société des Produits Nestlé, SA 1800 Vevey, Switzerland. Trademark holder: KIT KAT)

they see it as an original way of meeting customers at street events or pop-up stores. Unconventional viral approaches, on the other hand, seem to have drawn the attention of many marketing and communications actors since the term was first introduced by Jeffrey Rayport in 1996.[30] Yet despite these practitioners' growing interest in unconventional approaches rooted in outside environments, such approaches continue to be under-studied and under-conceptualized[31] by theorists. This is strange, given that more and more companies have opted to develop so-called ambient marketing campaigns. There are several reasons explaining this lesser interest in outside environment-oriented approaches:

- They benefit less from the rise of the Internet, which has considerably increased interest in viral approaches.
- They were long considered as mainly constituting a specific form of (outdoor) advertising.
- They are part of the experiential and sensorial marketing approaches that were so popular during the 2000s.[32]

Nonetheless, these techniques remain an excellent alternative way of promoting brands, as demonstrated in Table 2.4.

Table 2.4   Differences between Conventional and Unconventional Marketing

	Advantages	Drawbacks
Conventional Marketing	+ Publishers are resourceful professionals who do not wish to hide their identities + Quality control/editorial supervision + Mainstream exposure	− Expensive, requires considerable resources and high production skills, requires contacts, long lead times, etc. − Consumers can be elusive − Expectations are implicit, not explicit − Same media for everyone − Immobility − Consumer lack of interactivity/desire to share
Unconventional Marketing	+ Less cost + Greater recognition and awareness + Innovative and creative + Surprise and spontaneity effects + Build "sympathy capital," emotional connections + Easily understood + Mobility, connectivity	− Marketing window is shortened when the operation is not rebroadcast online − Possible lack of control, potential for negative buzz to have negative impact on credibility − Consumers may be anonymous

Table 2.5   A Comparison of Types of Marketing

	Relevance for				Efficiency				Convenience	
	NGOs	Young targets (15–30)	Luxury	New Technology	Performance/Impact/Results				Low budget	Little investment (HR, time)
					Short Term		Long Term			
					High	Low	High	Low		
Ambush Marketing	-	+++	+	+++	X		X		+++	+
Street Marketing	+++	+++	++	+++	X		X		+++	++
Stealth Marketing	+++	++	+	++	X			X	++	++
Viral Marketing	+++	+++	++	+++	X		X		++	++

McDonald's campaigns are worth scrutinizing for both their unconventional and their conventional approaches. The remainder of this chapter will provide managers with a guide allowing them to better understand these unconventional outside environment–oriented marketing approaches. It starts by defining them and highlighting their differences and ties to other leading unconventional approaches before going on to specify the main contexts in which they are applied and discussing possible future scenarios. Table 2.5 recaps this discussion.

THE REMARKABLE RISE OF STREET MARKETING APPROACHES

People are generally familiar with two unconventional outdoor marketing approaches, namely ambient and street marketing. Unlike street marketing, ambient marketing includes all variants of advertising, including the most traditional forms. It is based on the development of an external (or away-from-home) advertising, including traditional advertising that, in its most innovative form, can be transformed into an outdoor event creating the kind of atmosphere that is likely to engage consumers[33] in their urban meeting places. According to Gambetti (2010), such meeting places include the streets people use, the public squares where they gather, the places where they go to buy or consume things—all those occasions when they are most receptive to brand messages.[34] The problem is that in traditional away-from-home advertising, companies tend to use billboards on a massive scale. It is different with ambient marketing, which is happy to use any available physical surface to transmit messages, including manhole covers, cranes, pizza boxes, and free postcards.

In an ambient marketing campaign run for Frontline,[35] the antiflea product brand, bystanders found themselves at the heart of the action, since they were the parties giving meaning to the advertising effort. This is because, seen from the top of a tall building, pedestrians below resemble fleas that a dog wants to scratch on its back.

The term "street marketing," which Jay Conrad Levinson introduced in his first guerrilla marketing book, published in 1984,[36] involves companies benefiting from tools such as brochures, vouchers, or other kinds of flyers to promote their products and services. Street marketing's roots are the distribution of flyers and other samples. Following this, it began to be characterized by new constructs such as street culture and street art[37]—forms of external communications that mobilized a particular imagination that the street itself was transmitting. The best definition of street marketing has been developed by Jean-Marc Lehu, who views it as "a variant of marketing that, as its name indicates, situates its action in the streets, in the broader sense of the term, in order to generate direct contact between a brand, the elements and the marketing and/or communications targets. Very wide arrays of tools are used here, ranging from the simple distribution of brochures and/or free samples to major event communications operations."[38]

Even if the two approaches are similar today in terms of the way they are used to create outdoor events,[39] significant differences remain between ambient and street marketing approaches, with each meriting its own focus. The remainder of this chapter will therefore focus on street marketing, to avoid any confusion with conventional approaches such as billposting.

Main Differences between Ambient and Street Marketing

The fact that street marketing belongs to the family of unconventional marketing approaches has got certain observers thinking, by extension, that it "might also consist of getting groups of individuals to infiltrate specific locations in order to inform or influence certain representatives, identified as potential prescribers."[40] This confirms street marketing's many connections with other unconventional marketing approaches, including stealth marketing (witness the infiltration effects) and viral marketing (through the way people are influenced).

In addition, through its connections with street culture and street art,[41] this kind of marketing is often situated at the edges of legality (something discussed further in Chapter 8). It also requires a great deal of creativity. Among the main elements comprising street culture are rap and hip-hop, as well as a very distinct dress code, dictating many of the fashions in today's world. Street art is an artistic movement combining people who use posters, stickers, stenciling, paint, mosaics, and street furniture, or else who put on street shows (called busking) in urban spaces. What these artists have in common is their (legal or illegal) practice of using the city as their stage—something that, over the long run, may or may not transform the space in question, which tends

Table 2.6 Ambient Marketing versus Street Marketing

Characteristics	Ambient marketing	Street marketing
Basic action	Advertising on outside walls	Distribution of flyers
Action's location	All outdoors platforms	Mainly the street
Etymological reference	Ambience/Atmosphere	Street culture/Street art

Street Art Rules Applied to Communications

- Superseding ordinary platforms (flyers, brochures, vouchers, or other posters) and using new functional media such as urban furniture.
- Rewarding audiences instead of trying to persuade them.
- Redirecting advertisements to insert them into noncommercial messages.
- Stimulating the community's senses by inserting messages in unusual places.
- Getting the audience involved in co-constructing the performance (often using new technology).
- Linking a brand to its social context.
- Having messages that are incomplete because it is easier for people to reappropriate them.
- Finding comfort in associations with other brand messages.

to be the street.[42] In a sense, the street benefits from street marketing. It is a potential way of renewing communications.[43]

Lastly, street marketing's connections with street culture and street art have helped it to transcend a vision where the street is portrayed as a mere platform, so that it becomes a place whose very purpose is to stage communications.[44] This involves not only intervening at the level of the street per se but also using its culture and actors. It is an approach that positions street marketing as something particularly suited to the defense of shared values and social causes.[45]

THE EXAMPLE OF BEN & JERRY'S

The main communications constraints for a company like Ben & Jerry's are how to match its creativity with the need to attract people; how to spread a coherent message; and how to adapt to consumer expectations.

These very problems tend, in fact, to constitute the main challenges for many companies who would like to regain their attractiveness to a consumer base that is constantly evolving, in turn forcing companies to question their own communications methods.

The root causes underlying this dynamic reflect a veritable metamorphosis in consumer profiling. Possessing greater information about the products that they consume; grouping together in communities; willing to communicate via social media (which means having no compunction about sharing positive or negative opinions of a product or service); protected by organizations whose very purpose is to defend them; and demanding that companies treat them differently—modern consumers have become veritable prescribers capable of ensuring a product offer's success or failure in as much or as little time as they need to spread information about it using social media.

Modern consumers are actors with clear expectations. They want companies to be more transparent and work harder at developing communication strategies that stir things up. This means that today's consumers are asking companies to take better care of their needs, desires, and expectations, by refocusing their strategies around the consumers' own interests—which explains why companies are paying more attention than ever before to consumers' increasingly detailed demands. This is especially important given how easy modern consumers find it to betray once-venerated brands.

It is in this context that new communications techniques, including street marketing, have arisen. Many tools have been developed recently for the express purpose of touching consumers in their daily lives, surprising them, and helping them to break out of their routines. These are often fabulous techniques that also allow those companies that have yet to achieve significant market share to become better known, even as they develop a mindset that is as innovative as their bigger rivals—all because they are trying to highlight everything that they are prepared to do for their consumers. In the end, innovative techniques like these have become extraordinary means of differentiating companies from the competition, which has become increasingly difficult.

One example is Ben & Jerry's, a company born out of two men's desire to conquer one of the world's most competitive markets. Ben & Jerry's put its head above the parapet and has proven that a company can thrive when its products match what much of the population wants, and when this is associated with communications that are unusual but also enthuse the very same target. With its many innovative communications operations attracting more and more consumers and ensuring existing consumers' loyalty, Ben & Jerry's has, to a certain extent, been a revolutionary enterprise. To achieve its goals, the company has used the full range of alternative marketing tools. Whether this meant distributing samples, product placements at events sponsored by someone else, organizing street events, or developing digital platforms, Ben & Jerry's has been ready to do whatever it takes to succeed in a market that was not necessarily very hospitable. Today's entrepreneurs will stop at nothing.

There is an old proverb that "Sticks and stones may break my bones, but words will never hurt me." Ben & Jerry's have exemplified this, imposing its creative streak on a public that had not been asking for this. The example reveals the new communications concepts' attractiveness as well as the ways in which they open doors that were once tightly shut. Just ten years ago it would have been inconceivable for a company to attack the giants of the fast-moving consumer sector. In other words, the brand's success has as much to do with its innovative communications operations as with the quality of its products.

KEY POINTS IN PART 1—MARKETING TODAY

1. Alternative marketing exists because communications platforms improve from time to time.

2. This renewal is explained by consumer fatigue, brands' need to be exceptional, and economic crisis.

3. The empirical definition of alternative marketing, as opposed to traditional marketing, is based on two main ideas: originality and affordability.

4. Consumers are increasingly becoming actors who serve as brand prescribers.

5. Guerrilla marketing redirects the initial function of an object, decor, or location.

6. There are four types of unconventional marketing: viral, stealth, ambush, and ambient.

The Street Today

Chapter 3

Reimagining the Street

People have long been afraid of the street, seeing it as a place that is unsafe and where they might even catch diseases. At the same time, streets have always been places where people gather, because of all the sensational things happening but above all because they want to share or trade things and debate all kinds of topics, from the most mundane to the most serious. In ancient times, speakers would use public squares to harangue crowds of bystanders. In more recent times, these same spaces are used by demonstrations contesting many aspects of modern life. The street can be a place of negativity or positivity—but in both cases, there is no doubt that over time it has become the vortex of the human condition as well as a universal symbol of how lives can be shared. Everything is possible in the street. Anything can happen. The street can be as much a source of greed as of generosity; of joy as of fear; and of suspicion as of belief.

Then there is the ongoing change in the reputations attributed to streets. Whereas in seventeenth-century Europe, the street was viewed as a place of depravity, trash, rats, poverty, and misery, one century later it had already become a holy temple of commercialism. As for today, streets can best be analyzed as places where people can and do share things and ideas, and where they subscribe to a whole range of causes. The street has become the epicenter of human relations, whether this involves ideological demonstrations or commercial gatherings.

Clearly this sociological evolution is of great interest to marketing specialists. The first way of looking at it is to analyze the idea that streets are in the process of being reclaimed by certain organizations. Indeed, there is even a movement bearing this name. Subsequent analysis will then portray streets as commercial communications platforms, focusing in particular on a global phenomenon called (in the UK, at least) the Big Lunch.

RECLAIMING THE STREETS

In an era characterized by globalization and technological change—with more and more people living their lives vicariously online—the street has become a locus for opposition, where those who dispute this new civilization can meet to share things and express themselves.

As aforementioned, the street has always been a place where people can meet. This has evolved in recent years, however, culminating in new kinds of actions that are as original as they are innovative. One example from 1994 involves an antiestablishment UK direct action group called "Reclaim the Streets," which wants to reappropriate streets and public spaces. Its members have done things like organizing fake car crashes in the middle of London, with demonstrators suddenly appearing afterward to reappropriate the public space by setting up a coffee shop, sound system, tables, and chairs. These kinds of events have become a breeding ground for the anticapitalist movement that has grown in magnitude over the past decade or two.

Additionally, there was the global street festival held in 1998 in opposition to the World Trade Organization.[1] This movement, denouncing the values of capitalism, translated many people's sense that fun and street theater are much better than physical confrontation. Symbolizing a change in mores, this action was the trailblazer for an entire movement opposing the economic establishment. In the end it transmogrified into a veritable alternative political movement, giving birth to many others that would use the street as a symbolic theater for their actions, and subsequently as a platform for innovation, creativity, and the sharing of ideals.

People today no longer hesitate before descending into the street to disseminate whatever messages they hold dear. Examples of this new behavior are innumerable, including, most recently, the huge opposition between the advocates and opponents of gay marriage in France.

Irrespective of whether these ideological demonstrations are peaceful or not, they are all based on the idea of reappropriating the street and its values. After all, there is nowhere better than the street to rally huge crowds to one's cause.

As explained by Aventin (2006), the general idea here is to surprise people and turn things upside down at the very heart of their daily lives: "Urban life is full of all kinds of events that interrupt daily routines, which 'disturb' a space and its routines by altering people's rhythms and practices. In some way, such events tear people away from their routine perceptions and representations, destabilizing their daily experiences and ordinary patterns."[2] These demonstrations are meant as trailblazing combats in support of ideologies at odds with current values. The movements' oppositional aspect gives members an opportunity to assert their position and express resentment.

This is the logic underpinning the great wave of innovations spilling over into streets today. The only way that demonstrators can maximize the surprise they create and rally people to a common cause is to use tools that are both original and striking. Whether this involves posters, banners, situational role-plays, or even speeches, everyone is trying to find a way to distance themselves from daily routines and create a sense of surprise and curiosity. Hence the idea that the street is better understood as a space of innovation and freedom, where people from different universes mix with one another, gathering in tribes that share certain ideological values.

Aware of the power of the street, marketing specialists have understood that it makes consumers more likely to listen to their narratives—that is, as long as consumers can be interested in joining this encounter. This has given rise to a new trend, where marketing and communications spill over into streets and their main components. More than a simple place where people meet, streets have become commercial spaces where posters and flyers are increasingly replaced by urban furniture that is not always used for the purposes for which it had been originally imagined. This evolution of the street, converting it to a communications platform, has opened up new perspectives at the edges of globalization—oddly enough, considering that globalization is the very system that earlier movements were always fighting.

FROM MEDITERRANEAN *PASSEGGIATA* TO AMERICAN BROWSING

It is worth recalling that the street's original vocation was to help people go from point A to point B using bespoken infrastructure created toward this end. In this sense, streets lent themselves to *passeggiata* ("taking walks" in Italian). Yet, as noted above, this space has in the meantime also become a locus of commercialization, hosting a cornucopia of boutiques and storefronts whose only purpose is to attract consumers and get them to fulfill their main function: to consume. At the same time, it would be wrong to imagine that modern streets' sole function is to serve as a shop window. They do offer other opportunities, especially with the advent of new technologies facilitating the implementation of new marketing tools.

Thanks to the rise of geolocation technologies, the street has become a fully fledged commercial weathervane. Any street in any city worldwide can be viewed nowadays simply by going online. With tools like Google Maps, Google Street View, or Foursquare, travel has never been so fast or easy. It is only necessary to click on a few links to discover the whole of a city and identify its main monuments, restaurants, buildings—and stores.

Under the pretext of modernity and comfort, all kinds of applications exist today to facilitate the search for nearby shopping locations. It is no longer unusual to find applications referencing the best clothing stores, the most fun leisure centers, restaurants in all price ranges . . . anything and everything there is to be found in a particular neighborhood or street. Against this backdrop, the street itself has become a focus for business. Brands (and more generally, companies) pay geolocation specialists to ensure that anyone surfing online sees their product offer first, before their competitors'. The success of an application like Foursquare shows how powerful geolocation has become in the modern world. For many users, it is paramount that their friends and networks know exactly what they are doing and where they are going.

There has also been a change in streets' secondary function. Originally imagined as a place for taking walks, little by little streets have become platforms for online browsing. More and more people use digital navigation tools such as Google no longer just to discover historical monuments but also to find the specific kinds of stores they know they like.

Another sign of this functional evolution of the street is the rapid and impressive emergence of a new promotional approach called "wait marketing." The principle here is to take advantage of situations and locations where people are waiting for something, to expose potential consumers to advertising messages that use public furniture (benches, bus stops, places where people wait in line, etc.) as their communications platforms. Popularized in a book by Diana Derval, wait marketing hones

in on moments of relaxation where people are waiting for something—
situations that are often boring, hence conducive to the dissemination of
information, messages, or values.[3]

The advantage of this new communications trend is that the brand
can target an entire population. Everyone has times when they must
wait for something, be it a bus at a bus stop, in an airport, loading a
page online, sitting in a doctor's waiting room, etc. Marketing specialists
have looked at this and discovered that such moments lend themselves
not only to the dissemination of messages but also, and above all, to
their memorization by consumers.

Wait marketing also demonstrates marketing specialists' growing
interest in consumers' daily lives, which they increasingly use to disseminate messages and create a more direct connection with their targets.
In a world where everything happens very fast and where a multitude
of rival product offers creates a sense of flux that consumers can find
highly confusing, it is paramount that entrepreneurs be in tune with
their targets. Wait marketing gives them this opportunity, revealing once
again the street's importance in brands' strategy of refocusing on consumers' daily lives. There is nothing very surprising anymore about seeing brands invade urban spaces, which in this way are rapidly becoming
avenues of product democratization.[4]

In short, streets are spaces where all categories of people meet, interact, and share things. Streets are important to everyone, whether companies or consumers, bystanders or demonstrators. This can be seen in the
new kinds of demonstrations taking place in streets today, gatherings
that do not necessarily have a commercial purpose but try instead to
bring strangers together to share a unique moment. Examples are events
where hundreds of people suddenly appear in a public space to have a
drink. These kinds of happenings have become increasingly widespread
in recent years. It is worth taking a closer look at one in particular,
known as "the Big Lunch."

THE BIG LUNCH: A SOCIOLOGICAL EXAMPLE

The Big Lunch, which has recently started to spread across the United
States, is a modern version of a movement first seen in the UK for Queen
Elizabeth's coronation in 1953 and resurrected for her Jubilee in 1977.
First spreading across Continental Europe in the late 1990s, its catalyst
in this part of the world was the *Repas des Voisins* street festival scene
that grew organically out of Paris's 17th arrondissement. The basic idea
here is that one way to remedy growing isolation in large modern cities

is for neighbors to share meals, with everyone bringing their own food and drink to the table. In this way, neighbors who may not know one another can start connecting to their neighborhood.

In the French version, this street gathering—run every year the last Friday of the month of May or the first Friday of the month of June—has given birth to a rapidly growing movement that is officially supported by many politicians (including the country's association of mayors) and social institutions (like housing bodies), all of whom see it as a useful way of giving people the sense that they have a stake in their neighborhood. Indeed, the concept has become so popular that in 2004 the first-ever European Big Lunch Day was held, with more than 150 European cities organizing an annual street party day since then. The phenomenon has spread well beyond Europe now to include cities in Canada, Turkey, Africa, and elsewhere.

The growing success of this movement can be explained firstly by its communitarian aspects. In a world where individualism is on the rise, some observers feel that the only way of reshuffling the established order is for people to learn to share again, transcending the logic of individualism that often prevents our being open to one another. As noted by Blin, the concept's success can also be explained by the fact that it allows participants to reappropriate their streets: "Already, by physically occupying the street for however long the meal might last, neighbors are appropriating the reality of their space. The antitraffic barriers put up for obvious security reasons attest to the legitimacy of this appropriation of public space, one supported by municipal authorities. In a sense, it accentuates the privatization of the place."[5] The ultimate goal here is to create a possibility for individuals who do not necessarily know one another to share things, since they may very possibly have a joint interest in certain products, or else in a school, a political party, or just the neighborhood itself.

Whether or not organizers use social media to publicize their event, what they are manifesting here is a shared desire to break free of established societal codes by transforming a public space, whose use has previously been determined by a public authority or administration, into something open to everyone. The Big Lunch street party is a phenomenon representing the reappropriation of public spaces and additional evidence of how streets are emerging as important platforms for disseminating values, working much in the same way as street art, culture, or food—all approaches born out of the street and which use it to convey their own values and norms.

TRIBE AND STREET CULTURE

The preceding example typifies unconventional marketing, which has benefited greatly from the Internet and facilitated and intensified the viral aspects of these kinds of campaigns. This online dimension is becoming increasingly connected to an offline dimension that marketing specialists have started cultivating in unprecedented ways. Unconventional marketing focuses today on a space that has hosted many marketing specialists' most effective experiments, namely the street. Together with its culture, art, and tribes, streets and street-based marketing create conditions negating the conventional home/point-of-sale dichotomy that has traditionally structured the consumer experience.

THE STREET AS RAW MATERIAL

Streets are not just places that people use to travel from one point to another. They are also meeting places, as well as useful platforms for promoting things, ideas, and people. Along with this, they are also becoming spaces for affirming one's culture or tribal belonging. From happenings to street shows, people have started using the street to affirm who they are and what they believe in. Some marketing and communications professionals understand this and have started promotional campaigns that view the street itself as a raw material. This follows extensive studies of how streets have evolved as concepts, and what this means in terms of adapting strategies. The understanding here is that consumers have become bored with traditional marketing campaigns, which have unsurprisingly lost their impact, given how many ads the average person sees in an average day.

It is important to understand that using the street as a platform involves more than just passing out flyers to pedestrians. Using the substance of a street as a promotion and communications platform means connecting to people and showing them something new, exciting, and unusual. The purest example of the street as a substance is street art, where artists use the street as a platform for expression. Art is how they use their creativity to convey publicly their vision of society. By so doing, they rely on the full spectrum of emotions at their disposal. Their paintings, mosaics, billboards, or other forms of expression might utilize, for instance, humor, frustration, or anger. Through their works of art, these contemporary artists reveal the spirit of street culture, with street art itself becoming a way of developing alternative public discourse.[6]

A further example of how street expression evolves is provided by flash mobs, which are ephemeral meeting of persons who usually do not know each other, the aim being to carry out a predefined and coordinated action. Such actions take place in the street or other public places, giving participants an opportunity to affirm their desire to belong to a group. Flash mob participants are, in essence, expressing the power of "us," with the street being turned into a venue for communal expression.[7] Note that flash mobs are rarely political. What they signify instead is a desire to protest against the de-customization of public space. The experience of a flash mob constitutes a prototype of the postmodern consumption experience, insofar as it is uniform, fun, collective, and most importantly, co-created by consumers who transcend the role of observers to become actors in public discourse. In short, streets' emergence as both a raw material and a platform is more than a simple trend; it a true ethos inspired by street culture; an opportunity for consumers to affirm their membership in a group; and/or a chance for them to express their ideas, wishes, or feelings. It is clear to see how unconventional marketing has adopted various elements of street culture[8, 9]—inviting, in turn, reconsideration of the image of the street itself.[10]

THE CUSTOMIZATION OF URBAN FURNITURE AND URBAN TRIBAL CULTURE

As aforementioned, streets have become places of meeting and expression. More than that, they have become the principal venue of expression for consumers who wish to affirm their belonging to a tribe.[11] Indeed, most consumers use streets to show publicly that they are part of a group featuring common ideas, passions, or wishes. Companies and marketing and communications professionals have come to acknowledge that this "tribal era" might offer a real opportunity to create a direct connection to consumers. Indeed, tribal marketing has become one of marketing's most successful strategies today. Examples such as strategies promoting cosmetics for dark-skinned people or products targeting "nerds" or "geeks" respond to most consumers' desire to affirm their membership in a tribe. Numerous tribe movements have emerged over the past decade, a development that has forced marketing actors to adapt their strategies.

Marketing specialists have discovered that one great way of showing their interest in consumers is to encounter them down in the street. This has meant using unconventional marketing to develop micro-universes directly linked with their customers' habits and desires. One example from 2007 was the "Lomowall operation" in London's Trafalgar Square, illustrating how consumers can be encouraged to affirm their individualism. The project's success has significant ramifications for companies seeking to connect with customers by engaging them in self-expression. Through such operations, marketing and communications actors and their target consumers co-create a universe, forging strong links in the process. Brands, and companies more generally, can thus convey a sense to consumers that more than being mere targets, they can be real actors and ambassadors of the brands they love. This last point may partially explain the success of "brand communities" and is one the most important aims of unconventional marketing operations.

By customizing elements they find in the streets, brands are able to express their values, promote their products or services, and put consumers at the very heart of their communications strategies. Communication thus becomes experiential for consumers who take part in the moment, sharing a private link with the brand and with other consumers. Using spectacular or ephemeral activities,[12] brands produce memorable moments for consumers, who may go on to create a conscious or unconscious link between the moment and the brand that has been the agent of their positive experience. These spectacles are perhaps the ultimate form of consumer experience. They are, interestingly enough, already starting to change, insofar as they have become more open to consumer co-creation. These are instances where consumers collude with producers' formulation of their consumption experiences, resulting in more powerful and personally significant encounters. They play along with the rules set by marketing specialists, but only to a certain extent.

Street marketing is a compelling way of promoting a product or service by using familiar space—the street—thereby allowing the brand to form a personal connection with customers. Through these kinds of campaigns, consumers are becoming actors in brands' communications strategies, exercising power and creativity in the process.[13] Street marketing is thus a form of marketing that enables companies to use the street as a marketing workshop—that is, an effective way of introducing consumers to a brand's communications while transforming them into brand actors.[14]

UNCONVENTIONAL MARKETING CREATED BY CONSUMERS

According to Ritzer, Dean, and Jurgenson, "There were good reasons to contend that factory workers in the heyday of the Industrial

Revolution could be thought of as producers, and shoppers in the United States in the 1970s as consumers, but such thinking is embedded in, and limited to, specific historical circumstances."[15] Announcing the rise of "prosumers," these authors cast doubt on a central assumption of marketing that is a consequence of the economy, namely the idea that on one hand there is the sphere of producers, and on the other, the sphere of consumers. This convention is becoming less and less relevant. Today we can observe the rise of collaborative approaches mixing producers and consumers in the design and realization of communications campaigns and other brand events. And through such mixtures the approaches in question are being made unconventional.

The focus today is no longer on doing marketing *about* consumers ("market to") but rather on marketing *with* consumers ("market with"), as prescribed by the Service-Dominant Logic of marketing.[16] Consumer–producers (or "prosumers"[17]) are an increasingly important phenomenon in contemporary consumption and society.[18] This has clearly been supported by the increased usage of the Internet, especially World Wide Web 1.0 and 2.0; consumers have become highly empowered through their relationships with companies.[19] This has caused them to produce their own interpretations of meaning and strategy associated with the brands they prefer.[20]

The general understanding now is that thanks to the Internet, consumers have become more powerful and creative as subjects, with this new modus operandi having a knock-on effect on their consumption and how they use the market. Indeed, the very act of consumption has become an area where consumers are able to exercise power and creativity.[21] This means that consumers are now producing meanings that are not always expected or predicted by brand strategists.[22] Indeed, consumer–producers sometimes go on to generate their own brands that they then spread widely using World Wide Web 2.0 technologies[23] like Firefox, Geocaching, or Linux.

A number of research streams have looked at the active role that consumers play in the market. Such studies often deal with very different aspects of actual consumption practices, however, and tend to be rooted in different theoretical backgrounds.[24] Most relevant here is the literature that has developed in the field of innovation management,[25] examining end users' role in this new product development process. The initial focus had been on the role of lead users, small groups of subjects whose collaboration has been purposefully sought and exploited by companies from various sectors because such users are more active and creative and can serve as opinion leaders in their respective communities.[26]

Later, a more general approach was developed, in which scholars broadened the scope of their analysis to include communities of end-users and consumers who collaborate with (often large) companies in developing new products.[27] Examples can be found in the field of consumer products (sports-related communities such as NikeTalk) and professional equipment (electronic music production forums like the Propellerhead company website). In this view, consumers can act as both developers and marketing specialists, contributing to new products' success by shaping functional characteristics and using their position as opinion leaders and trendsetters to enhance market access.

STREET BRANDS

Brand communities are in rapid expansion, such the well-known United States brand Harley Davidson, which has already fascinated market specialists everywhere. Likewise Europe has Ducati,[28] whose management model has allowed them great success. Ducati has become Europeans' current darling motorcycle—as well as a cult brand with followers called "Ducatists."

In Ducati's business model, its staff and consumers become a brand community with the same status. They belong to the same community. On one hand, brand products are consumed by staff members, and on the other, the idea, accessory, and event producers are the consumers themselves. Thus, the classic example of brand community lies with Ducati and the Ducatists. They reflect the true partners for the company's emergence in the context of consumer-producers.

This erasure of boundaries between consumers and producers is clearly very much in fashion, as witnessed notably by the consumer-generated content approaches[29] that Web 2.0 has popularized, and co-creation concept introduced the new Service-Dominant Logic marketing theory.[30] The situation has changed from "market to" customers, to "market with" customers, following increasingly popular marketing patterns. Consumers and companies will be co-creator of values.[31] Brand communities have pushed the concept of "marketing with" to the limit, insofar as virtual platforms are being created for brands.[32] This has helped create unity between staff members and consumers who have the same passions.

This has given rise to collaborative approaches, through which marketing is evolving into true participatory conversations around the brand.[33] According to Hatch and Schultz, "Branding is now recognized for its ability to create dialogue inside organizations (for example, between functions) as well as between members of the organization and its customers, consumers, fans and critics."[34] The boutique consultancy Trendwatching coined the term "Customer Made" to define this phenomenon of "corporations creating goods, services and experiences in close cooperation with experienced and creative consumers, tapping into their intellectual capital, and in exchange giving them a direct say in (and rewarding them for) what actually gets produced, manufactured, developed, designed, serviced, or processed."[35] Examples include Dell with its initiative Idea Storm: Where Your Ideas Reign, Starbucks with My Starbucks Ideas, and LEGO with Lego Factory.

"Unconventional marketing" is a term that describes transformational approaches that seek to turn entrenched assumptions of marketing on their head. The first wave of unconventional marketing, associated with guerrilla marketing, confronted the convention that the impact of a communication campaign should be directly proportional to the budget invested. The second wave, associated with street marketing, broke with conventional wisdom that marketing is confined to a home/point-of-sale dichotomy. The recent third wave, concerning consumer-made products, confronts a prevalent marketing convention derived from the economy itself: the separation between the production and consumption spheres. The present chapter has shown the revolutionary impact of each of these waves of unconventional marketing, and how this impact persists in mainstream marketing practices.

Chapter 4

Where the Street Generates a Modern Culture

The focus in this chapter is on how popular and spontaneous street culture has—by transforming itself into a fashion—become a source of business and given birth to a global market.

STREET CULTURE

Alternative (and more specifically street) marketing derives from urban culture. Brands have descended into the street to meet consumers in their daily lives, reproducing the most ubiquitous urban codes in their efforts to reach their targets. But they have also learned to take advantage of the notoriety of new and globally famous street muses, having them carry their products and use their services. Well aware of these new stars' enormous powers of persuasion (notably among young people), brands have developed products matching the values that the stars publicize, all of which is very attractive to young people today.

One example might be accessories brands looking to market new headphones. What could be better than showing some famous footballer or other sportsperson wearing the product? This system has demonstrated its effectiveness, for instance, in the market for tennis shoes, sports shoes often worn by American rappers, many of whom are real urban icons. Their fans imitate them, but even more significantly, trainer sales now go well beyond the comparatively small circle of urban music fans. Indeed, it is not unusual nowadays to see men or women in business clothing wearing them as well. Sales have exploded, with brands now looking to break these products down into different ranges. Tennis shoes that are no longer only used for sporting purposes have long been a real symbol of belonging to a wider group. For the person wearing them, they attest to his or her membership in a particular tribe of consumers.

Street culture is omnipresent, in music and fashion but also in art and luxury goods. This helps to explain the current success of new street communications trends that use codes characterizing these places, and which consumers dip into on a daily basis.

STREET ART

Street art is another essential component of urban culture. Note firstly that this is not a new art form, in the sense that it was already being practiced in ancient times. It consists of using urban platforms and elements as tools for conveying messages or simply expressing artistic meaning. Street artworks have the advantage of being visible to a very large public.

Aware of the growing popularity of these forms of art, some companies have taken advantage of the opportunity they represent. Examples include advertising in the form of graffiti on walls, on the ground, or in train stations. Street artworks also have different vocations. They can be ideological, exemplified by the outcry caused by the sight of polar ice caps melting due to global warming; or political, like the iconic "hope" image associated with Barack Obama's first election, which ultimately became the candidate's official poster. Other artists who get noticed because of the poetry of their work have been approached by brands asking them to use their art to promote certain products. Examples include IKEA turning to one of the world's leading graffiti artists, Banksy, to promote its product designs.

Street art uses techniques as diverse as stenciling, mosaics, posters, graffiti, or painting. Its main codes are shared by the vast majority of the population. Globally it has become a widely used means of expression, and one that is closely connected to street marketing. Nowadays, it can often be applied directly in the staging of street marketing operations.

STREET EVENTS AND FLASH MOBS

Flash mobs have become an essential pillar of today's alternative communications strategies. This kind of operation constitutes a deep trend, consisting of groups of individuals gathering in a public space for very short period of time, focusing on items as varied as politics, education, businesses, or the audiovisual. Agreed in advance, such actions are aimed at creating mass operations that will then be widely broadcast online. Flash mobs can take on many different forms, including dancing and other kinds of innovative theater.

One example is the flash mob that gathered to pay homage to Nelson Mandela, upon his death in 2013, in a supermarket in Pretoria.[1] Another was the giant choreography honoring Michael Jackson, organized by prisoners in the Philippines in 2009.[2] Flash mobs have broadly arisen in the shadow of the Internet, which now features sites dedicated to this form of communication. Social media is also important to flash mobs. Indeed, it is mainly using such tools that participants find one another. Flash mobbing's success has led to the rise of other similar forms in recent years, including freezing, carrot mobs, *métroteufs*, kiss mobs, zombie days, pillow fights, Harlem Shakes—or, in fact, any kind of commercial gathering whose purpose is to advertise something.

Freezing happens when a group of individuals suddenly freeze in place for a few moments in a public place. Carrot mobs are sudden actions where consumers all debark at a specific point-of-sale to spend their money there. In exchange for the extra sales made during such events, the outlet agrees to changes to its processes and materials—for instance, to become more environmentally friendly.

A *métroteuf* is a party held in a subway train and lasting as long as a round-trip journey. Akin to freezings, kiss mobs involve chains of individuals kissing one another on the cheek. This form of communication arose in the wake of a campaign to raise awareness of and compassion for people with HIV-AIDS. The idea was to get HIV-positive people to go into the street and ask strangers for a hug. It was an original way of showing that AIDS cannot be transmitted in this way.

Zombie days, inspired by Michael Jackson's famous "Thriller" music video, are events where participants disguised as zombies and behaving like them parody people who generally behave badly. Street pillow fights are sometimes huge events involving people of all ages. They have proliferated to such an extent that a league has been created in Canada, with April 9, 2009, having been proclaimed the first annual International Pillow Fight Day. Lastly, "commercial gatherings for advertising purposes" consists of people getting together to promote a company's products and social services.

Today, although most companies and organizations across the world no longer have any compunction about using these different federating forms of communication, the idea is not necessarily to promote a product, service, or brand but to demonstrate participants' desire to share moments of fun with other people. A simple fad at first, flash mobs and other street spectacles now symbolize a desire to transcend individualism in an attempt to share, exchange, and discover things.

All these street actions share a common purpose, which is to generate as much buzz as possible to disseminate a message, idea, or ideology. One example is the globally recognized organization Greenpeace, which uses the street all the time to spread its message.

THE EXAMPLE OF GREENPEACE

Greenpeace is an environmental campaign group with a global presence, organized globally into twenty-eight national and regional offices. This nonviolent, international NGO takes great pride in its independence from any state body. It considers itself free of all ideology and simply denounces anything that damages the environment, while offering solutions that help to protect the planet and promote peace.

Greenpeace appeals to audiences on an unprecedented scale, in large part due to the creativity of its actions. The organization understood very quickly that only quite shocking actions would be able to give it sufficient visibility to get a large number of people interested in the causes that it is trying to defend. This explains why its members were so quick to adopt new communications technologies, referred to generically as "alternative marketing."

Greenpeace uses meetings of state representatives to organize its own demonstrations. At the 2009 G8 Summit, for instance, Greenpeace members placed a giant balloon representing an iceberg in Paris's River Seine. The balloon deflated little by little, reminding people of the polar ice caps melting. The aim was to raise general awareness and put pressure on decision-makers meeting at the same time at an international summit in Aquila, Italy. The NGO's members were aware that this kind of action would be widely aired in the media, which would rebroadcast it on a grand scale. Greenpeace has made such forms of communication during high-profile media events one of its preferred modes of action, thereby becoming a seminal actor in what has come to be known as ambush marketing.

A term invented by Jerry Welsh,[3] "ambush marketing" can be defined as all the marketing techniques that an organization uses to increase its visibility by taking advantage of an external event (clearly, in order to be an ambush, the organization will not have helped to fund said event).[4]

Benefiting from the publicity associated with this big event means that the ambush organization will necessarily gain notoriety. Ambush specialists' creativity has often been able to draw the mainstream media's attention away from the original functions (conveying information about the event itself), with the ambush operation becoming the new focus, despite being unfunded. The success of such actions explains Greenpeace's preference for the technique and the likelihood that the NGO will resort to it again in the future.

Chapter 5

The Street and Word-of-Mouth

Buzz marketing is another alternative marketing technique. Often assimilated with viral marketing, it is a communications strategy based on word-of-mouth, the idea being for a company going online to disseminate a promotional message that attracts consumers who will then relay the same message to their own contacts.[1] It is also a way that a brand can improve its image and notoriety. Different tools have been developed to implement this process.[2]

Brands are well aware that social networks constitute excellent dissemination channels, if only because they are almost completely free of charge and comprise millions of consumers. Companies have been taking advantage of this situation to develop their social networking presence and create more direct connections with customers and/or prospects. Most companies today have Facebook and/or Twitter accounts complementing their website. These digital platforms help them to appeal to a new public, ensure existing customers' loyalty, and differentiate themselves from the competition. In the world of digital communications, creativity is key. It is a value that helps companies to surprise consumers they meet online, who will then be more likely to disseminate the information in question. It is worth remembering that the main objective of buzz is for consumers to appropriate part of the company's strategy, becoming actors instead of spectators. By disseminating the desired message, consumers themselves become the pillar of this communications strategy.

In addition to social media, companies use their digital presence to amuse, surprise, or shock consumers. By creating online games, interactive platforms, or participative strategies, they can build new relationships with consumers. These ancillary tools are more direct than traditional advertising and make it possible to build on word-of-mouth, enhancing a company's chances of maximizing its returns from digital investments.

Some companies have increased their notoriety via a single viral campaign, surprising Internet users and helping them to transform a virtual experience into an unforgettable one. Becoming brand spokespersons, consumers quickly relay information to their personal networks, enabling them in turn to enjoy an experience that is both fun and original.

Buzz can build very quickly. Sometimes it only takes a few days or even hours for a digital campaign to cause a major buzz. The easiest way of achieving this with modern platforms would appear to be by measuring the strategies' impact. For this, it suffices to look at the number of people who view and/or participate in an action to determine its operational reach.

At the same time, buzz is not necessarily quantifiable. Hence the need, before starting to design an operation or campaign, to ensure that Internet users will enjoy the time they spend online. In an era of consumerism and mass lobbying, it is not enough for companies to trust their luck. Creating and generating a buzz requires organizational competency and adaptability. It is not enough to simply launch an idea or an original concept online and hope that people will like it. The buzz must be nurtured, with the campaign's actors being encouraged to disseminate the information intelligently.

Indeed, this might be the greatest challenge, given the need to find a proper balance between encouragement and visual enthusiasm. Messages can, for instance, be updated without these necessarily troubling consumers. If a message is repeated too often or overpowers, consumers might reject it—and, in the most extreme cases, spread negative buzz about the campaign. Hence the importance of finding a good balance and building a buzz matching target Internet users' habits and desires.

In addition, to achieve a quality buzz, it is essential that companies consider the campaigns their competitors are waging. Something that has already been seen will never generate as big a buzz as something original. Yet even though breaking with the past could be the right choice, it is also a risky way of proceeding, if only because it is harder to calculate how Internet users might react to a concept without any precedents. If companies looking to adopt this approach had just one rule to follow, it would be never to take for granted all of the different factors involved in creating and sustaining a buzz. This is a delicate strategy—but one that can be highly profitable if properly controlled.

MAXIMIZING INVESTMENT RETURNS

The question then becomes how to measure return on investment once a street marketing operation has been implemented, especially in a context defined by the huge economic crisis that the whole world has faced in every sector of activity since 2008. Advertising's heyday—which peaked in the 1980s—is long gone. Alternative marketing has become the leader among brands' new means of communication. Street marketing, born out of guerrilla marketing, has come to epitomize small-budget operations for brands seeking to develop a creative image that people will notice.

It is worth remembering how much it costs to run a page of advertising in a national publication or a one-minute spot on a national TV channel. A thirty-second primetime TV commercial might, for instance, run $150,000. Compare this with a street operation whose images can spread globally online for less than $1,000. The "Scratches on your car" ads run by online insurance specialist Novocortex cost around $1. The idea in this global campaign was that urban mobility itself can be used as a marketing tool. At the same time, it is extremely difficult to calculate ROI for this kind of campaign. Estimates might be determined along two lines: quantitatively and qualitatively.

Quantitative Measurements

Singer Christina Aguilera's perfume was launched in Israel with a campaign that saw thousands of hangers scattered across the country's streets, each holding a perfume sample with the slogan "Sometimes it's all you need to wear." The operation was so successful that the product sold out within eleven days. A similarly noteworthy operation on the French Riviera saw "Luxury brigades" walking through the streets handing out vouchers (that looked like tickets) enabling people to buy jewelry in Paris's Place Vendôme shopping district. Consumers would be able to present their ticket to the sponsoring stores to enjoy a discount, making it easy to measure the operation's quantitative impact. Indeed, when campaigns use traditional platforms such as flyers, measurements are always easier.

A further example was the Japanese luxury brand Kenzo's Flower perfume campaign, when the company planted up to 150,000 poppies

Photos 5.1 and 5.2   The Novocortex Street Marketing campaign, "Scratches on your car." (Used by permission)

in the courtyard of Paris's Pompidou Center. Within just a few days, all points-of-sale in the surrounding neighborhoods ran out of the perfume, symbolized by a poppy. According to the brand director, sales rose by 100 percent in four days. In this kind of situation, it suffices to measure product sales immediately following the street marketing operation's launch. If revenues are up without other operations running at the same time, it might be concluded that the street marketing operation explains the difference in outcomes.

A further example involves the large German candy maker, Haribo. For twenty years, the company has organized street marketing operations in European capital city train stations, re-creating a waiting room atmosphere replete with massages, see-through sleeping pods, and candy vending machines. To increase journalistic buzz, it has also rented buses and parked them in front of newspaper offices and radio stations. The buses offer the same atmosphere as the train stations, including massages. After these two-step operations, during which something like 80,000 products will be handed out over a period of four days, brand sales tend to increase by something like 13 percent. This more or less satisfies the sponsor's ambitions, exemplified by the statistic that out of the 450,000 persons using the Auber subway station in central Paris every day, up to 200,000 came face to face with Haribo's operation, meaning that they saw the brand and noticed what it was doing.

As aforementioned, it has always been very difficult for companies to quantify the impacts and benefits of an unconventional communications campaign like street marketing. It is worth recalling that actions of this kind improve a brand's notoriety and visibility in public and private spaces, one example being when the NGO Misereor offered street bystanders a chance to slide their debit cards into an interactive panel so they had a sense of virtually slicing a loaf of bread—the strapline being "Yours is the gift that feeds."

The current crisis has forced companies into a cost-cutting mode, adding to the popularity of low-cost creative unconventional campaigns. Previously, street marketing had suffered from a major disadvantage that made companies hesitate to use it, namely the absence of measurable outcomes. Entrepreneurs need to quantify their ad campaigns, calculating how much they cost and what they bring in. One original example of this might be an inexpensive communication recently chosen by a hair salon in England.[3]

The question here is calculating how many people actually saw this customized street furniture—hence, its conversion rate (the number of people purchasing a product or service following a particular marketing operation). To do this, key guerrilla marketing operation performance indicators have to be determined. The principle is simple and would involve bystanders leaving their personal details (on the spot or online) to help build up a commercial database full of facts enabling ROI measurements.

Mail Metrics, a specialist CRM agency belonging to the Key Performance Group, is a partner of LCA Street Marketing for a "Drive to stand" B2B operation that ran on September 23, 2014, at the Paris E-commerce fair. Individuals dressed as security officers offered guests false €500 banknotes (in a process akin to the distribution of flyers). The reverse side of the note featured four-figure codes enabling recipients to open a safe located at the Mail Metrics stand, with successful participants receiving a CRM solution valued at €2,000. The only way people could get one of these notes and take part in the process was to leave their business card. About 3 percent of visitors to the fair showed up at the Mail Metrics stand, totaling 1,200 persons. The conversion rate was then calculated based on the number of sales divided by the number of business cards handed in.

In marketing, it is crucial to measure a campaign's ROI. This helps to relativize investment costs in terms of their yield, often defined by the revenues they generate. Recent interviews with talented SMEs such as Birchbox or Depiltech, or large firms like ACER, have shown that these companies' marketing directors prefer traditional market actions rather than unconventional creative ones. This is because street marketing's originality precludes quantitative estimates being produced before operations actually run (due to the fact that, by definition, such actions are more original and unique than are traditional marketing strategies).

Abu Dhabi's Falcon Construction, for instance, has found a way of diving headfirst into street marketing, but with a guarantee of quantitative results. The company, which was selling thousands of apartments near Casablanca, Morocco, called upon the services of LCA Street Marketing. The agency distributed thousands of keys across the streets of Morocco, inviting recipients to open a door potentially giving them access to the apartments for sale in Casablanca. People could only participate, however, by leaving their details with local salespersons, building up the company's commercial database. This street marketing operation (involving the distribution of keys) was "monitored" from beginning to end, so that management knew exactly how many keys had been distributed, how much the operation cost, and how many apartments were subsequently sold.

From "below the line" street marketing to "above the line" media

Fiat's marketing team recently told Professor Bernard Cova, who works closely with me, that the main reason so little use had been made of alternative communications campaigns lay in the absence of reliably measurable results. One response might be to allocate annual budgets ranging from €5,000 to €15,000 to so-called "below the line"[4] unconventional

Photos 5.3 and 5.4 False banknotes used in a Mail Metrics campaign, run during the Paris E-commerce fair in 2014. (Used by permission, www.streetandmarketing.com; www.lcaconseil.net)

street and other guerrilla marketing operations. It then becomes easy to turn these operations "above the line," since it suffices that the data be monitored. Images of street marketing's renowned KitKat chocolate candy bar bench operation have gone around the world. Yet despite its innovativeness, there have never been any figures measuring the impact on KitKat sales. This is the kind of thing that must be changed.

A final example of how street marketing data and outcomes can be tracked—this time in a very different sector—relates to the VTC service offered by Nice Road, which is like Uber but more upmarket. Present in Nice, Monaco, Saint-Tropez, and Cannes, the company launched a street marketing operation in October 2014, with a team of fake chauffeurs in Cannes' more affluent streets distributing new French drivers' licenses bearing the Nice Road brand colors. Bystanders were given an opportunity to avail themselves of Nice Road's VTC services by uploading an application using a QR code and then applying a discount code. Combining the two tools with an innovative street marketing campaign, Rochdi Akbi, Nice Road's MD, was able to monitor the operation's conversion rate: 4,500 licenses (actually flyers) were distributed, with around 100 persons uploading the application over the following days. Similarly, the number of people signed up to Nice Road's Facebook page rose by 8 percent during the period of the operation.

Photo 5.5   The Kit Kat candy bench. (Courtesy of Société des Produits Nestlé, SA 1800 Vevey, Switzerland. Trademark holder: KIT KAT)

Now that street marketing's ROI can be calculated, its future is promising. A successful street marketing operation today consists of combining low-cost creativity with several key performance indicator tools (QR code, online data mining, etc.) to analyze how successful a campaign is. Armed with this arsenal, there is nothing stopping entrepreneurs from adopting the new approach.

Qualitative Measurements

Another way of measuring such operations' return on investment is qualitatively. Above and beyond their financial returns, street marketing operations can also help to improve a brand's image and renown. Yet this kind of ROI is much harder to assess than its quantitative equivalent. It can only be measured over the long run, as brands and consumers move closer to one another. In other words, the key here is increasing customer loyalty.

A street market operation is always more effective (and, above all, more relevant) than a traditional advertising campaign. Given that the former costs less, it becomes possible—with an identical budget—to carry it out a grander scale. Moreover, given the growing saturation of the world's advertising space, street marketing operations are becoming a better way of reaching people, making it easier to attract consumers' attention by going out to meet them where they live. Street marketing helps to solidify consumer loyalty in both the short and the long run. Short-term, street marketing helps to reach people who do not yet know the brand. Long-term, it creates a veritable community with consumers because they are living new experiences with the brand.

KEY POINTS IN PART 2—THE STREET TODAY

1. The growing use of street marketing and reappropriation of public spaces is based on a changing vision of the street. At first, this was negative. Today, it is more positive.

2. Streets can be vectors of ideals and places for ideological expression as well as gatherings.

3. The street's original role has been transformed into a space for commercialization.

4. Alternative (and particularly street) marketing derives from urban (or street) culture, whose codes it tends to reproduce.

5. Often assimilated with viral marketing, buzz marketing corresponds to increased word-of-mouth regarding a communications strategy.

6. Today the Internet is the main vehicle communicating the buzz that starts in the street.

7. The main goal of buzz is for consumers to appropriate part of a company's strategy, becoming actors instead of spectators.

Street Marketing

Chapter 6

An Evolving Practice

According to Levinson, companies can use street marketing weapons (such as brochures, vouchers, posters, etc.) to promote their products and services.[1] In this vision, street marketing is a less-expensive alternative to conventional marketing. Today, it has become autonomous from guerrilla marketing to a degree that would have been unthinkable thirty years ago when it was first formalized by Levinson. Its development is specifically indebted to European countries, starting with France and Italy, where it is construed today as a full-fledged marketing approach in itself.

This third section will describe how street marketing has changed over the years, first by trying to define the practice; then by studying specific case studies (the Mini, Thierry Mugler, and Azzaro); and lastly by looking at how it is used elsewhere.

INCREASINGLY USED BUT POORLY DEFINED

A great many websites describe street marketing as a marketing technique that uses the street and public places to promote an event, product, or brand. In general, it tends to hand out event-related materials, ranging from tracts or flyers to different and more original forms of billposting. The same definition tends to be found in layman's texts in this field.

A broader academic definition might view it as "A subset of marketing that, as its name indicates, situates its action in the streets in the broader sense of the term, seeking to generate direct contact between certain elements and marketing and/or communications targets, on one hand, and a brand, on the other. Wide arrays of tools are used, ranging from the simple distribution of brochures and/or free samples to the organization of major events-related communications operations."[2]

Many companies are fully aware of these techniques' advantages and use them more and more often. This notably involves international brands that no longer hesitate to turn to the new tools as their main communications platform or as complements for more expensive campaigns. Companies like the Mini, Orange, McDonald's, and Microsoft have all adventured into alternative communications. Nonetheless, this type of campaign is not the sole reserve of the corporate world, with street marketing also being widely used nowadays by NGOs such as Amnesty International and Greenpeace. The purpose of such operations is to surprise customers in the places where they tend to spend time. Some organizations even use street marketing operations to convey political or ideological messages.

Paradoxically, despite becoming increasingly widespread, street marketing operations remain relatively few and far between. The academic world, for instance, is not very familiar with them. Indeed, many communications professionals are unfamiliar with the specificities of each type of street marketing operation, possibly due to ongoing vagaries in their classification. All may share the property of using creativity to attract and/or surprise consumers, but with new and increasingly creative campaigns appearing every day, grouping them into specific techniques is very complex indeed.

Note as well some companies' reluctance to resort to these new communications tools if too much time has elapsed since they first appeared—possibly because managers are afraid of looking like simple followers lagging behind leaders who had applied these techniques from the outset. Even so, it is highly likely that these same companies will try to use the new techniques at some point in the future in order to avoid being criticized as has-beens. Indeed, companies in some markets where such forms of communications had never found a foothold are starting to rely on them now. McDonalds, for instance, recently engaged in an unconventional sundial technique to promote its new breakfast menu. The message that the brand offers here is that each hour of the day has an appropriate snack.

In another example, the French DIY chain Mr. Bricolage had dozens of trucks repainted with trompe l'oeil "paint pots" across France. The objective of this operation was for the trucks to surprise motorists with a touch of humor. This transformed its trucks into a powerful communication medium.[3]

Street marketing has not been entirely democratized yet. The situation can evolve, however, given how many companies are finally becoming aware of the very real opportunities that this new communications technique offers.

THE EXAMPLES OF THE MINI, THIERRY MUGLER, AND AZZARO

The increasing frequency with which street marketing is being used can be partially explained by the way it enables original communications campaigns at a lower cost, while creating more direct connections to consumers in more horizontal kinds of relationships. Additionally, street marketing can be used to improve a company's image.

One example is the Mini, a mass-market automobile brand facing tremendous competition. By offering consumers a fun and original product range and by opting for different kinds of marketing operations, the brand has succeeded in promoting its cars while conveying an image that is different from its rivals (and more innovative than them). In using these campaigns, the brand wants to emphasize its creative and innovative side, as well as its proximity to customers. It is trying to surprise both prospects and customers alike, even as it continues to listen to them and respond to their needs. Customers have become increasingly demanding but will recognize these efforts, meaning that they will start to improvise as these companies' ambassadors, disseminating their communications using their own social networks.

Mini is one of the companies that have fully understood how questioning its own communications strategy would allow it to optimize its image and consolidate its existing customer base while also attracting new clients. Hence its efforts to implement a number of different kinds of alternative marketing communications operations—one of the most successful examples being when it built a roundabout in the middle of Paris made out of its Roadster models.

Another example of a company ready to invest in unconventional marketing is the Clarins Fragrance Group, which recently asked a laboratory specializing in marketing consultancy and new communications concepts to think about implementing street marketing operations for its Thierry Mugler and Azzaro brands. The consultancy's mission was to determine as precisely as possible these two brands' personality and values, from their creation until today. It did this by studying all of their advertising and then undertaking a thematic analysis of interviews with employees.

Once this identity was defined, the consultancy came up with original ideas for street marketing operations connected to the companies' values. This started with creativity sessions, followed by groups focusing on how well the new ideas fit into a particular context. Out of this brainstorming came more than three hundred ideas for operations. Unsuitable ideas were eliminated by the participants themselves, who were also given the possibility of choosing which ones they found more appropriate. Then came a debate culminating in the establishment of two specific categories, the first listing the most original ideas, and the second those that were easiest to implement. By crossing these two categories, the final choices were made in terms of which operations should actually be launched.

It is worth recalling that the purpose of this mission had been to find an original way of optimizing the brands' visibility to its existing customer base while attracting new clients as well.

This was not the first time that the Clarins Frangrance Group had tried street marketing, having previously resorted to this technique to promote its line of cosmetics. For this earlier experience, it had chartered a bus that traveled across France to try to get bystanders to participate in a product demonstration, following which they would take away free samples. The operation's success encouraged the brand, followed by other brands in the group, to return to street marketing.

The Clarins Frangrance Group example shows that the success of street marketing is mainly linked to its ability to adapt to many different brands and sectors of activity, including luxury goods. At this point, it would be useful to look at how street marketing has been used in a non-French context.

OVERVIEW OF PRACTICES ACROSS THE WORLD

Specialists consider that street marketing practices have been revitalized by new technologies capable of conveying and amplifying these creative actions beyond national borders.

Human Events in England

Examples here include street teamers, who invest a space that then becomes their medium. The goal is to demonstrate the product or service as it is being used. One example is Lush, an English company dating from 1995 that develops and markets cosmetics entirely manufactured from organic and fresh fruits and vegetables. These natural products are handmade and have an appearance that corresponds to the brand's a differentiated image.[4] They also have a particularly unique quality, which is that they come without any wrapping—or on those occasions when they are wrapped, they only use recycled materials. To promote the brand's organic nature and lack of packaging, employees in all of its boutiques are encouraged once a year to take their clothes off in a campaign called "ask me why I'm naked."

Road Shows in the United States

Mobile visibility is a variant based on the use of transportation. One example saw the American shipping company FedEx[5] create the illusion of transporting in one of its trucks packages bearing the label of its main competitor, UPS, while stacking much smaller UPS trucks on FedEx's own vehicles. It should be remembered that comparative advertising is allowed in the United States, as is "denigration," whereas in France it has taken a while for these methods to be accepted. The message here was that no one is quicker at making deliveries than FedEx. Thanks to truck road shows, everyone could see this advertisement; that is, the audience was much bigger than would have been the case with a traditional billboard. But the operation cost much less.

Disguised Actions and Stealth Promotions in Israel

As stated in the previous chapter, the campaign launching the Christina Aguilera perfume involved strategically scattering around a number of public spaces hundreds of hangers carrying nothing but a sample, exhibiting the slogan, "Sometimes it's all you need to wear."

Giant Karaoke in London

In 1999, a giant karaoke event was organized in Trafalgar Square by the telecommunications company T-Mobile, working with advertising agency Saatchi & Saatchi. More than 13,000 persons gathered, without realizing that the singer Pink would also be there to perform. The mobile operator had distributed microphones to participants, with their voices being rebroadcast while cameras filmed them and retransmitted the images on a giant screen.[6]

Event-related actions of this kind can also come in the form of games or open contests, which might be run all across the world. One example is the famous annual Red Bull contests, dirt biking championships organized by the brand with its recognizable bull logo.[7] Details are provided below about how these street marking operations are put together.

Chapter 7

Creating a Street Marketing Campaign

Although creativity and originality lie at the heart of street marketing, it is not enough to have a good idea and implement it, to be successful. Carrying out a street marketing campaign requires real know-how and specific competencies. To optimize a campaign's chances of succeeding, the operation must first be analyzed strategically before implementation. This involves a benchmarking study determining the brand's direct competitors in terms of communications and promotional strategies. This stage helps identify which operations have already been carried out, thereby avoiding situations where the operation is designed like (and/or copies) something that has happened before.

Following this stage, companies must undertake an exhaustive study of their targets, and more specifically their core targets. Such studies consist of contacting the brands' consumers, carrying out a consumer satisfaction study, and then getting in touch with the managers of the stores that will be distributing the brand's products. Care must be taken at this level to complete all of these stages and underpin them with qualitative and/or quantitative studies.

Following these investigations, which help to determine more precisely what brand consumers expect from it, brainstorming sessions are organized to develop as many relevant ideas as possible. This culminates in different kinds of classifications (financial, creative, feasibility, etc.) that help to identify which ideas are most creative and provide the best fit for what the investigating company is looking for.

The greatest challenge is then to establish precisely the main strategies enabling operationalization, while reflecting upon the segmentation-targeting-positioning strategies and the operation's geolocation. Lastly, technical, legal, and financial feasibility studies of the operation are carried out, followed by a forward study of the campaign's impact, notably in terms of the word-of-mouth that it is likely to generate.

Subsequently, a more operational phase will see the chosen strategy's implementation. This phase comprises three main steps: identifying the best idea; looking for the most suitable media platforms; and selecting subcontractors to carry out the operation. These three phases will also have to be included in the strategy's total budgeting. That is, the street marketing operation also includes a number of external costs relating to different ancillary strategies: buzz marketing, press relations, Internet relays, presence on social media, or determination and development of a gaming strategy involving the creation of SMA online games helping the buzz to last once the operation is over.

The final stage is the front-line operationalization. This is the endgame. It includes all of the previous strategies and helps catalyze a generalized qualitative buzz.

It is clear now that devising a qualitative street marketing strategy requires particular competencies and not just a good idea. Other evidence for this includes the rise of communications agency specializing in this field; the advent of new professions aimed at optimizing such strategies; and many professional or academic specialists' growing interest in this topic.

CREATIVITY SESSIONS

Carrying out a street marketing operation requires good organization, a clear brief, and adherence to an approach that is both exhaustive and complex. This is because the actual operation is nothing more than an endgame, the conclusion of a strategic effort that the investigating teams will have defined in its smallest details. Before initiating this phase, it is important to find ideas that are sufficiently original to reach consumers—but also doable and in sync with whatever constraints (e.g., budget, brand values) the company has determined must be in place. There also needs to be a direct link with the company's aspirations. It is at this level that creativity sessions have a role to play, enabling the emergence of many new ideas, including ones that will ultimately give birth to the final operation.

To ensure that a creativity session takes maximum advantage of participants' potential, certain behaviors are required. Firstly, session participants should organize a brainstorming period lasting a few minutes. Osborn has established four main rules for this activity: criticism is forbidden; enthusiasm is encouraged; quantity is an imperative; and there must be a systematic search for combinations and improvements. The idea is to encourage all participants to take part and come up with as many ideas as possible (with one agreeing to minute the proceedings). The ideas that emerge will then be reread and undergo a discussion-debate to get rid of any that do not adhere to the rules and constraints that have been specified. The remaining ideas will be classified in terms of their originality and feasibility. By crossing these two classifications, the best ideas can be chosen—meaning the ones that are easiest to implement.

Cutting-edge communications consultancies have developed creative processes conducive to the emergence of original ideas for street marking operations. Examples include one-day brainstorming sessions aimed at developing original and relevant operations capable of optimizing a particular brand's street visibility. Toward this end, a team of colleagues gets together, comprising people from different departments (who are therefore likely to provide different viewpoints). The conditions must be relaxing, so that each participant feels at ease, freeing their imagination and creative juices. A note-taker is chosen randomly and given the job of jotting down everyone's ideas, even the craziest ones. There must not be any censorship, even self-censorship. Moreover, no feasibility or budgetary constraints should be imposed at this juncture.

A trained moderator (often the person deemed to be the most creative) will represent the company and guide the group into different situations, some of which can be frankly outrageous, in order to relax everybody and get them to open up. On occasion, participants may wish to verbalize certain ideas, including the most absurd ones germinating in their heads. If so, it is important to classify all of these ideas in different tables. A range of categories might be developed, including ones involving, as an example, urban furniture customization ideas, the distribution of flyers, etc. The purpose of this classification is not to establish constraints likely to restrict participants' creativity or inventiveness. Instead, they are there to organize ideas around different lines of communication, thereby maximizing the number of alternatives those customers will be offered.

It is important that the sessions be organized for three different kinds of audiences:

- Potential brand users
- Current users
- Company employees

A few principles need to be established at the beginning of the session:

- Principle of incompetence or positive competence: participants consider that they know nothing because they want to avoid imprisoning themselves in a narrow mindframe, the hope being that they will then come up with more ideas.
- Principle of deferred judgment: whether the ideas that come out of the brainstorming are good or bad will be judged at a later date.
- Principle of distance: trying to move away from one's corporate role to gain a bit more perspective during the creation phase.

A number of rules must also be determined:

- The need to be freewheeling (spontaneous and creative)
- The need to be prolific (expressing a maximum number of ideas)
- The need to combine (leveraging whatever ideas are suggested, i.e., enriching/ modifying/mitigating or simply associating the latest idea)

The session starts with an illustration of the principle of incompetence. This might include a question like how many floors a cat can fall without necessarily hurting itself (the right answer in this exercise, coming from a Boston hospital, is 34). In one instance when this question was asked, none of the session participants guessed more than ten floors—allowing the moderator to stress the principle of people knowing how little they know and using this knowledge to enhance their creativity.

The principle here is to come up with a maximum number of ideas. These will then be sorted (for instance, in a table) in terms of their feasibility, relevance, and originality. The one hundred best proposals are kept. At the final cut, the three most doable ones will be retained. (See Table 7.1.)

Table 7.1   Filter Table

Ideas	Feasibility	Budgeting	Coherence with Targeted Positioning	Relevance
Idea 1	+++	+++	No	Yes: +
Idea 2	++	+++	Yes	Yes: ++
Idea 3	+	+	No	Yes: +
Idea 4	+++	+++	Yes	No

Once the creativity sessions are completed and the operation chosen, the brand must present its objectives and plan of action (the operation's geolocation, etc.). This means drafting a brief.

DRAFTING BRIEFS

A good example here is the British streetwear brand ZOB, which asked the Nouvel'R consultancy to organize communications celebrating the upcoming opening of its Paris store with an operation corresponding to its image—that is to say, a street marketing operation.

Context

- 2008 saw the brand's launch in France, with its first store opening in the country (featuring a floor space of 800 square meters in Paris's 9th District).
- ZOB: A British underground prêt-à-porter streetwear brand known for working with the pioneering street artist Banksy.
- ZOB wanted to be better known by (and attractive to) new French customers between the ages of twenty and thirty, fans of the street art clothing concept.

Aims

- Communicate the launch of a clothing line carrying the Banksy logo.
- Communicate the opening of ZOB's first store in France.
- Raise the targets' awareness of the new concept of a store dedicated to street art.
- Develop the brand's notoriety among a target of early adopters in Paris and France.

Campaign

- Flyers
- Stickers
- Happenings
  - Tags written in chalk in shopping districts
  - A dummy half-buried in the ground
  - Operations run by two persons stopping bystanders and distributing flyers

ZOB Campaign Figures

- 54,400 flyers distributed
- 3,000 stickers placed
- 204 hours of actions in the field
- 74 persons working on the operation and directly representing the brand
- 16 operations run in Paris's most visited districts

Here are a few key principles when preparing an action plan leading to a successful operation:

- Consumers must be directly involved in the advertising.
- Consumers must be surprised by the operation.
- It should be original and fun.
- It should make it easier for consumers to encounter the brand.
- It should cost little compared to big media purchases.
- It should ensure proximity to (and a sense of complicity with) consumers.
- It should complement traditional campaigns.
- Participants' motivation can be controlled by a mystery shopper.

To be avoided in these front-line actions:

- Overly specific geographic targeting
- Consumer rejection or saturation
- Communications in the street but nowhere else
- Illegal operations

What needs to be planned for:

- Bad weather[1]

EXAMPLE 1 OF DRAFTING A BRIEF: URBAN BEACH

Urban Beach is a streetwear brand offering freestyle sports clothes and accessories (skateboarding, roller-skating, scooters, surfing, etc.). The brand owns different stores, including one in Nice, France, on whose behalf the brief below was drafted.

Company Details/Scenario at the Beginning
- The French market for sliding and gliding sports is new in this region.
- Urban Beach wants to put together a street marketing operation.
- Urban Beach should be positioned as participants see it—that is, not as the brand's employees see it.

Aims
- Devise a street marketing operation for the French market.
- Build the brand up in the street.
- Disregard budget or feasibility constraints. Everything is allowed!
- Creativity team comprising four to six persons (mixed group in terms of age, gender, nationality, etc.) plus a note taker with a computer. Each person has one piece of paper.

Table 7.2   Sociodemographic Criteria of People Participating in Brainstorming

Age	18 to 30	8	100%
Gender	Male	5	62.5%
	Female	3	37.5%
Professions and socio-professional categories	Student	4	50%
	Employee	4	50%
Education	Undergraduate degree	4	50%
Place of residence	Urban area	12	100%

Audience and Operations (Table 7.2)

- Revolving audience of eight persons
- Sessions all run in one day
- Four consultants and four students (recruited in Nice) to enhance creativity
- Two moderators

EXPLANATION OF GAMES AND CREATIVITY EXERCISES

Brainstorming (11 to 15 Minutes)

A traditional corporate brainstorming session lasts a few minutes. The famous American researcher Osborn had five rules for this: criticism is forbidden; enthusiasm is encouraged; large quantities are imperative; and there must be a systematic search for combinations and improvements. Within this framework, participants can be asked to describe what they think street marketing operations should look like.

Trailers (10 Minutes)

This game consists of using the brand's identifiers to choose a word or image randomly, and then starting with this word to imagine a scene from daily life. The note-taker jots down the strongest ideas and images. The moderator encourages feedback from everyone to shape the concept.

"Total Recall" or Role-Playing (20 to 30 Minutes)

This creativity exercise (which tends to be very popular among participants) was invented to encourage people to use their imagination to drive useful small changes. Participants might be asked to choose a new identity and write up an identity card with at least five basic details (first name, gender, age, nationality, family situation). A member of the group might play the part of a journalist and ask participants to imagine small changes in a brand. An initial introductory question describing the product might then help these "virtual consumers" to assume their new identities.

Reverse Dynamics (10 Minutes)

This technique consists of playing devil's advocate with the general direction of research. Participants start by describing a static product that might never evolve. They then go on to imagine all the small changes that they would hate. Hyperbole is encouraged.

Creativity and Urban Furniture (10 Minutes)

A second brainstorming session integrating the additional constraint of fitting in with existing urban furniture (including monuments) to ensure that the campaign is truly bound to the streets.

Screening of Ideas

Something like 500 or 600 ideas tend to come out of these creativity sessions. Depending on which street marketing operations have already been run elsewhere in the world, around 100 will be selected.

The case below demonstrates how to formalize these creativity sessions. Urban Beach, a slide and glide sportswear and accessories brand, wanted to carry out an alternative marketing operation to optimize its visibility. It turned to an agency called streetmarketing.com. Readers will find below the transcription of some of the ideas that came out of this project.

CONSIDERATIONS IN THE URBAN BEACH STREET MARKETING CAMPAIGN

Flyposting and Sampling: The Most Traditional of All Street Marketing Actions

- Distribution of wax samples (to wax down surfboards).
- Get people to bathe in the public fountains in the city of Nice, France, in swimsuits bearing the brand name, while distributing flyers. Some suits or accessories should be offered to anyone who agrees to jump into the fountains as well.
- People wearing swimsuits distributing flyers on the Nice city tram.

Mobile Actions

- Twenty people wearing swimsuits crossing the city carrying surfboards, looking like characters from a French surfing movie made in Nice. The surfers then take people to the store selling the product.
- Wet T-shirt contest: around a dozen young women wearing the brand's swimsuits and white tank tops showing the store's logo on their chest walk around carrying water and asking bystanders to splash them.
- Youngsters on skateboards hanging on to trams, carrying banners in the brand colors.

Product Events: Creating Temporary Spaces to Promote a Product

- Beach volleyball match organized in the middle of the city. Teams wearing the brand comprising bystanders and models.
- Mini-pool with waves built so bystanders can try a bit of wake boarding.
- Everyone encouraged to try their boards in the municipal fountains. Any bystander who so desires given a chance to try to stay on the board.

Event Actions: Happenings or Flash Mobs

- Organization of skateboard competitions involving different youngsters trying to win points. The audience judges the winners.
- A stand built on the beach next to the shopping mall where the "community" of Beach people meet (sailing school).
- Catwalk of swimsuit models. Bystanders asked to grade them.
- Freezing operation. Around fifty people carrying banner with the brand logo and store address comes to a halt in the main town square.

Undercover Marketing: Disguising Urban Furniture

- "Urban Beach" billboards set up across the city at strategic locations, the aim being to guide potential customers toward the store.
- Customized parasailing featuring the brand logo and store address.
- A temporary wall resembling a wave built near tram tracks, making the trams look as if they are going through a blue tunnel resembling waves. The brand logo is visible.
- Municipal fountains colored in blue.

A second example of a creative brief might be Thierry Mugler, a famous global brand in the prêt-à-porter fashion and cosmetics markets. Like Urban Beach, the brand wanted to use alternative marketing to emphasize its innovativeness, ensure its visibility, and differentiate itself from direct competitors. To achieve this, it also called upon streetmarketing.com, which, among other services, drafted a brief on the company's behalf.

EXAMPLE 2 OF DRAFTING A BRIEF: THIERRY MUGLER

Thierry Mugler is a leading prêt-à-porter clothing and perfume brand. The particular perfume in question here is Angel, whose packaging is represented by a star.

Type of Operation

Event action, happening.

Pitch

The campaign's idea was to build a giant slide connecting two highly visited streets in Paris (with one variant being to decorate a rooftop, showing angels flying in the open). Accomplices disguised as angels would float around this giant slide throwing out stars (made of soft materials) symbolizing the brand. Alongside this, hostesses dressed in Thierry Mugler would distribute Angel perfume samples to bystanders walking underneath the giant slide.

Operations' Relevance to the Brand's Positioning

The campaign seemed adapted to its target and the brand's positioning, which played on the product's symbolic value (the hedonic value of perfume, relating to the pleasure it gives consumers). In addition, the image of an angel in the sky fit the brand's intrinsic values, replete with mysticism, an image relating to luxury but also to dreams.

Music/Staging

A video of the event could be accompanied by soft music reminding people of the product offer, namely a trip to a world of dreams (with the words of *Ange* by the French singer Akon a good choice for the flying angels). The front of the screen would show angels moving up and down the giant slide, with the reactions of bystanders in the background. The images would swap back and forth for around one minute.

Expected Impact/Brand Impact

The brand impact could be very positive, inasmuch as the campaign would relate directly to universal values such as dreams and hedonism. The expectation would be for a qualitative improvement in consumers' image of the brand. A well-executed campaign could give consumers the sense of a brand really trying to get close to them.

Expected Sales Impact/Notoriety Objective

A widely broadcast campaign should be able to generate a positive buzz. This would accentuate the brand's notoriety rate among the consumers participating in the operation or watching the video. The strategy should also have an impact on sales, notably in the points-of-sales surrounding the places where the operation would happen.

References to Other Operations

The idea of the giant slide, with its excellent visual aspects, had already been used by Adidas for its "Adidas in the air" operation in Tokyo, and to promote the 2010 Vancouver winter Olympic Games (with men and women dressed in sportswear walking down a giant slide).

Complementarity between Media and Viral Platforms

Thanks to the video accompanying the campaign, it is clear that the operation would benefit from excellent complementarity between media and viral platforms and would have no problems being rebroadcast. Being shown online at DailyMotion, YouTube, Facebook or Twitter, the video would be quick to create a buzz—if only because street marketing had never experimented with this concept before. Given how creative this campaign was, it quickly became a reference in street marketing. And to increase the brand's chance of quickly enjoying a high-quality buzz, it seemed useful to send a copy of the video to the specialist viral and street marketing blogs, including the famous Alternative Marketing Blog edited by the Tribeca advertising agency.

Campaign's Philosophical Vision

This street and viral marketing campaign was a perfect fit for the values that Angel conveyed: mysticism, dreaminess, and luxury. By playing on these values, Thierry Mugler was also able to play on consumers' need for self-esteem. Such as it had been imagined, the campaign was meant to communicate the message that purchasers could get closer to their "ideal self." As mentioned, one of the main virtues of perfume purchasing acts is that they satisfy buyers' quest for hedonism. This kind of product is a self-indulgence, allowing consumers to express their desire for recognition and fulfilment (in the sense of Maslow's pyramid). It is therefore at this level that the brand should intervene, since this can become the cornerstone for a major customer loyalty/attraction strategy.

Problems

Security was an unforeseen expense. Many bystanders found it difficult to identify the advertising message. The brand therefore had to create more traditional communication platforms to complement its street marketing campaign.

BUDGETING

A street communications campaign requires precise budgeting to avoid last-minute malfunctions. Each cost must be controlled, and the budget must be aligned with the brand's aspirations. Street marketing does not have a predefined budget level (consultancies can work on projects ranging from €5,000 to €300,000), but it does generate certain minimum costs, albeit ones incomparably lower than for traditional media.

Firstly, to have a clear overview of the project, the objectives must be precise, selected carefully using the tools that will later be mobilized to achieve these objectives, assessing and justifying each expenditure corresponding to each one. Spending items must be assessed as rigorously as possible, if possible by organizing bid processes. The bids received should then be represented as the lower range of the budget—that is, the minimum numbers. It is important to get exact bids and ensure with the different counterparts that their numbers are clear and realistic. Vague costings must be avoided in street marketing—otherwise the risk is that the budgeting process will be skewed and the outcomes unrealistic. On the other end, an upper-range budget should also be established, incorporating more expensive counterparts' bids as well as contingencies in case of unforeseen or underestimated expenses.

The budget might be broken down into five main spending categories:

- Design/creation/execution
- Project piloting
- Production
- Gifts
- Production costs

Table 7.3 Brand X Budget for a Street Marketing Operation

A. Designs, Creation, Execution (Global)				
Concept and Creativity	Quantity	Units (days)	Unit Price	Subtotal
B. Pilot Project (Global)				
Media and Communications	Quantity	Units	Unit Price	Subtotal
Project Manager (two sites daily)				
Pre-op Comms Relay, Online and Offline (fixed price)				
Post-op Comms Relay, Online and Offline (fixed price)				
Community Management (fixed price)				
Press Relations (six months) (fixed price)				
Buzz (mobile platforms, six months) (fixed price)				
Dissemination of Videos and Media Complementarity (fixed price)				
Content Creation for Buzz (six months post-op) (fixed price)				
Customer Targeting w/ Buzz to Gain Loyalty (fixed price)				
Graphics Creation and Sensory Identity (included)				
C. Production				
Transport or Shipment Costs	Quantity	Units	Unit Price	Subtotal
Flyer and Banner Creation				
Flyer and Banner Printing				
Staff Time on Site				
Staff Outfits				
Film Crew (sound, lighting, video)				
Film Material Rental				
Operational Budget				
Transportation Vehicle and Drivers				
D. Gifts and Samples (if applicable)				
	Quantity	Units	Unit Price	Subtotal

Table 7.3 (*Continued*)

E. Insurance, Legal Fees, Other Fees				
	Quantity	Units	Unit Price	Subtotal
Insurance				
Legal Fees				
Licenses and/or Registration Fees (if applicable)				
SUBTOTAL				
TOTAL COSTS				

Subsequently, it becomes important that the budget also show the sources of income (and not only of expenditure). Income can come from partnerships, sponsors, or any other pecuniary inflow helping to balance the budget (see Table 7.3).

THE EXAMPLE OF HAYARI

The chapter finishes with a case study covering the initial phases of a campaign to the final buzz. Working with students, a consultancy undertook a study on behalf of the Parisian luxury firm Hayari, which specializes in haute couture and perfumes. All of its customers for both business lines are women. At the request of the company executives, the study focused on the perfume business.

Hayari wanted to become more visible in the United States and asked an agency for a strategic marketing study and different alternative marketing operational ideas. But instead of merely applying this advice, the company opted for a veritable communications strategy, including a street marketing campaign chosen from different proposals, involving the development of different communications platforms. Being cautious, the consultancy built an entire strategy based on the creation of an avatar for the brand, which it called Mister H. This meant that the brand could see what the outcomes might be without there being any direct impact on managers' choices, notably in terms of the long-term image of the brand that they wanted to convey.

Before choosing one operation over another, the consultancy carried out an exploratory study interviewing fifty women. Thirty-five responded, giving their view of the brand and more precisely of the perfumes they were shown. The study helped to identify different values, facilitating proposals that were then presented to the managers.[2] The findings helped to ascertain the suitability of the operations being suggested, which ranged from spreading white flowers in a large fountain in New York City to simply distributing personalized flyers. The end result was a classification organized around feasibility, originality, and impact.

Three of the ten best ideas ended up being implemented. This happened in New York City during the month of May 2014: on Madison Avenue; at James Fountain; and in Union Square Park. Two years previously, there had been a trial run in Paris. The location chosen seemed coherent with Hayari's brand image, since most bystanders corresponded to the company's target.

The first action in Paris had consisted of distributing perfumed flyers and personalized balloons. Afterward, the agency realized that it had not chosen ideal locations, since 80% of the women taking the flyers and balloons were not French. Also, bad weather meant that foot traffic had been low. Having said that, participants' general feeling about the perfume and operation had been positive.

The second operation was an event action—that is, a promotion outside of the point-of-sale—involving, in this case, a treasure hunt. The idea was to encourage participants to find an object relating in some way to the brand's fragrances. The first to do this (who found a bouquet of white flowers) would be awarded a bottle of Only For Her. The others would receive a personalized T-shirt. Despite a few negative aspects (relating, as always, to cold weather discouraging certain bystanders and reducing foot traffic), the proceedings suited the brand's image, with more than 60% of all participants finding it suitable and 29% very suitable.

In short, even if the weather and number of participants worked against the event action, its underlying idea was a good one. Indeed, everyone who took part said they had a good time.

In the end, the decision was made to organize a third more "undercover" action.[3] Originally, the letter H was supposed to be stenciled on the ground alongside James Fountain in the middle of New York City's

Union Square Park. A message would also be added: "Meet at 2 PM at the fountain." Balloons carrying the same message were hung from the fountain in question. Trees surrounding the square were used to hang personalized T-shirts bearing the letter H on the front and "Only For Her" on the back. Note that the idea of stenciling was dropped because authorization was not received in time. In the end, only five T-shirts were handed out, also because authorization had not been received that clothing could be hung from the trees.

Although it could no longer be considered as an undercover but instead as a street operation, there was still coherence with the brand's image and with the company's preferred codes (femininity and elegance). It was also an opportunity for the brand to increase its reputational capital and benefit from a word-of-mouth effect.

Each of the three operations were photographed and videoed, culminating in the production of three films, one for each operation. These then became the basis for a complementary media strategy. Later a Facebook page would be created, posting a whole array of photos and films. The page could also be used to simply click on an icon and order a card bearing the fragrance of Only For Her, a functionality that was widely commented upon and praised. A video of the overall operation was also published on YouTube.

The fallout from these different operations and actions was extremely positive. The number of Facebook fans doubled just three days after the operation (and rose by another 50% within a week, thus up 150% in total). The complementary media strategy did more than simply publish photos, videos, and posts, with many articles being uploaded onto the fashion pages of popular websites such as MyLittleParis, Marie-Claire, Cosmopolitan, or Perfumes. All of these articles were massively linked via Facebook.

Note, finally, that this communications strategy was also very effective in terms of reaching its core target—and this despite its relatively meager resources.

Chapter 8

Generating Buzz

Not all operations happening outside of points-of-sale involve street marketing. Street marketing is generally considered to comprise no more than seven techniques: the distribution of products and/or flyers; product events; human events; road shows; uncovered actions; and event actions.

DISTRIBUTION OF PRODUCTS AND/OR FLYERS

Street marketing has updated the age-old marketing practice of handing people brochures or samples with countless new actions that can be assimilated with this approach, ranging from people exiting a concert being given Lu Chipsters cookies, to patrons of a roadside diner receiving football-shaped binoculars stamped "Danone." Even more sophisticated is the relatively new practice of handing out so-called flypacks—combination flyers (pamphlets, brochures) and packs (packaging, envelopes)—containing product samples. This latter practice has become particularly widespread at festivals and evening outings.

One example of this is an event promoting Neutrogena hand lotion, in which the company had the idea of leaving flyers on scooter handles instead of giving them directly to bystanders. This made a lot of sense, with the flyers reminding two-wheeler drivers that if they do not wear gloves or other gear they will need Neutrogena's product.

Similarly, in 2007 the BBDO advertising agency had the idea of using suction cups to attach product samples bearing the Mercedes logo onto the hoods of rival brand vehicles, with a card saying "Enjoy your test drive" and a list of Mercedes dealerships.

A study has shown that 70% of all flyers distributed by brands are thrown away without being read. This may explain the decision by Neutrogena, Mercedes, and other brands to use street marketing actions to innovate. One case in point is when a leading mobile telephone company had the idea of handing bystanders a brochure that was wrinkled and torn. Recipients were so surprised to receive advertising in this state that they unfolded the paper to see what was written on it. A similarly original sample operation was conducted by the Columbian plastic surgery clinic Clinica Marquez, together with the SSA Laicon marketing agency, with a model wearing a T-shirt with "Before" written on the back and "After" on the front. Note that the woman had had breast enhancements, making her body itself into the operational medium. There is no limit to the degree of innovation found in street marketing.

PRODUCT EVENTS

The idea of product events is to come up with a temporary space that can be used to launch a new product. Possibilities include stands where people can try on shoes; counters where different kinds of ice cream can be tasted; or even hot air balloon launch platforms shaped like Nivea deodorant sticks. The general sense of these operations is to use a physical platform to promote a product that has signature status and/or has only recently been marketed. The aim is to get organizers to interact with bystanders by giving them a chance to talk about brand products or services.

For instance, to promote the launch of their new operating system, Microsoft marketing specialists had the idea of opening up a coffee shop dedicated entirely to the brand. This quickly became a meeting place for customers proud to say that they belonged to the community of PC owners.

The product event concept means finding a location where the product is available so that consumers might experiment with it. Nutella, for instance, celebrated one anniversary in Italy and Germany by inaugurating concept stores where visitors could taste Nutella-based products. Similarly, in 2007 Vans (a skating shoe brand targeting customers between the ages of fifteen and twenty) commemorated the invention of its signature waffle shoe by cooking waffles shaped like shoe soles and handing them out to people walking by in the street. Apparently a corporate VP helped to cook the waffles!

HUMAN EVENTS

Human events are operations in which companies call on so-called street teamers to take over a space that will then serve as their media. The goal is to show the product or service as it is used. One example is the apartments that Ikea built in the streets of Stockholm, creating theaters where, throughout the whole of the operation, spectators could watch people under normal living conditions.

In 2011, Europcar achieved good buzz online thanks to a large-scale human event operation thought up by the Ogilvy & Mather agency.[1] The idea here was to hang around parking lots, waiting until drivers left their cars and started walking away; as soon as their backs were turned, their cars were towed and replaced by "squashed" compacted junk heaps resembling their "former" vehicles. People's first reaction was to get really angry, especially once street teamers disguised as security staffers started insisting that cars were unnecessary in today's world. Owners were duly relieved once they realized that the prank operation was to promote Europcar's AutoLiberté rental agency. Following the campaign, visits to the Europcar website increased threefold. Indeed, the month of the operation in question, the company's YouTube sites were the world's fifth most visited.

The main advantage of these kinds of operations is the way they make it possible to present a life-sized product or service in its original shape. Consumers can identify immediately what the advantages are of buying the product. Such operations mobilize different factors. Firstly, the company benefits from street teamers' skill at attracting attention. Also, using the element of surprise gives brands a particularly positive image. Lastly, due to imitation and idealization effects, consumers witnessing the products or services' life-size presentations have no problems imagining how they might be used in real life.

ROAD SHOWS

Operations known as road shows revolve around new means of transportation—including bicycle rickshaws, Segway personal transporters, and showcoms (screens that event organizers cart around, broadcasting digital content). One example from 2001 was when Garnier organized a bus to drive around city streets, bearing the colors of its Fructis Style shampoo. Similarly, in Canada in 2005 there were the scooter parades that Vespa cleverly organized in the streets adjacent to the University of Toronto campus. The idea is to take advantage of new moving surfaces to enable bystanders to become both spectators of an action and protagonists driving it. The end result is direct contact between event organizers and consumers.

Many brands have opted for this form of communication because it enables different levels of visibility, depending on how organizers choose to operate. One recent example was when Conforama got people motoring around on Segway personal transporters to hand out discount vouchers to pedestrians walking up and down the French Riviera. This was an effective way of distributing across a wide geographic area. In another event, Nissan used an optical illusion to promote its new model, creating a poster stretching the entire length of a train[2] to create the impression that its new 350z sports car was as powerful as a high-speed train engine.

Less successful was the Subaru Impreza campaign that gave audiences the impression that it was promoting a type of glue—the idea being to emphasize the new "Subaglu's" ability to hold the road, by putting a tube of glue at the heart of the operation. Insiders would have found this clever, but the message was not clear to everyone. Clarity is a basic requirement of all successful street marketing campaigns. If people do not understand at first glance what the message is—as happened with Subaru—the campaign will fail.

A positive example from 2010 involved a four-week operation in Paris promoting the blockbuster movie Clash of the Titans. Buses driving through the city's entertainment and movie theater districts gave the impression of being squeezed to death by giant serpents. A similar operation was run in Copenhagen about the same time, by Danish agency Bates Y&R, the aim here being to promote the local zoo.[3] This type of public transportation–based road show can be particularly profitable, if only because a bus (or any other means of transportation) is capable of touring city streets any number of times, meaning that it will be seen by countless people, some without realizing how often they are seeing it. This expands the audience considerably. The cost might rise, but it is always less than a traditional media campaign.

Road shows can also center on people. Vancouver's Rethink Communication agency caused a buzz in 2009 by having an extremely hirsute man promote Parissa depilatory wax strips by walking the city's beaches in a swimsuit. Visibility was extensive, as was the online buzz, with holiday makers all pushing to have their picture taken with the man.[4]

In 2008, underground apparel brand Zoo York carried out a similarly high-profile action in the streets of New York, marketing vintage punk clothing styles to skateboarders. The campaign promoting the company's latest line, menswear119 (called Zoo York Roaches120), had a group of skaters seemingly putting cockroaches—part of the brand's logo—into their backpacks. They would then skate quickly around the Wall Street business area dropping cockroaches on frightened bystanders. The daring punk aspects of this campaign ensured its buzz.

In 2011, Thierry Mugler created the Womanity Bus to take advantage of new mobile units in promoting their perfumes. The campaign was to use the surfaces and mobile units to allow passersby to become both spectators and actors in the heart of the action. This facilitates direct contact with the consumers. Many brands opt for this kind of communication, as it can benefit from a scalable visibility dependent on the method taken by the facilitators.

Note that road shows can also involve technical platforms (buses, planes) as well as human ones (tattoos) and animals.

UNCOVERED ACTIONS

The idea behind uncovered actions is to transform the way urban furniture is used. One example from 2005 saw the Ubi Bene agency envelop Paris's Statue of Liberty in a Nike Tony Parker T-shirt. Several lessons can be drawn from this case. Firstly, many street marketing operations have a hidden side, in the sense that their commercial dimensions are not always made apparent. Secondly, as demonstrated previously, they often pursue an ambush approach, with urban furniture being used for something other than its original purpose. The main goal of undercover techniques, however, is to take advantage of a highly visible product location so that as many potential consumers as possible can visualize the attributes of a brand's product or service.

Actions of this type are very popular in street marketing at present, since they cost little and can be very profitable. One example was the extremely inexpensive "Acne: Don't pop it. Stop it" campaign that Impact Plus ran for the Dubai Health Agency in 2009,[5] involving little more than bubble wrap placed on a model's photo to create the illusion of a pimple. Windex, the household cleaning product brand, did something similar when it stuck seemingly dirty and opaque strips on the walls of a bus shelter[6] to communicate the benefits of using its products. This kind of highly original action can give a brand global visibility, as long as it is followed by an adapted buzz strategy.

Non-profits also employ this type of communication to raise public awareness and provide information about the causes they are supporting. One example is the advertising that Amnesty International produced in collaboration with the Barcelona agency Contrapunto BBDO, sticking posters of electric chairs above bus shelter benches in Spain to raise people's awareness of the scale of capital punishment globally.[7] Likewise, in 2010 the Abbé Pierre Charity Foundation used the forecourt of the Louvre Museum in Paris for a sensational operation, making a figure of a homeless person out of ice to remind visitors how few shelters are available in the summer. The slogan was "The homeless die as often in summer as in winter. We need to act."[8] The statue got the message across to everyone who saw it.

A further example comes from the New Zealand city of Auckland, which decided to start a street marketing campaign raising awareness of how streets can be dangerous for pedestrians, using the slogan "Don't step into danger."[9] The idea was a response to the more than nine hundred pedestrians who had been accidentally injured in the city over the previous five years.

Other campaigns not requiring any major investment include K2R, the famous stain removal brand, which drew pictures of clothes around road potholes to highlight its message, "Try K2r."[10] Similarly, in 2010 the Swedish furniture giant Ikea placed pieces of furniture in three Paris subway stations so that people waiting for trains could sit on Ikea sofas instead of the usual benches.[11]

Last but not least, in 2009 a particularly original campaign by the prêt-à-porter brand GAP—targeting young urbanites between the ages of twenty and thirty-five, a group who tend to be more favorable toward subversive actions—saw everything turned "GAP Upside Down" in the company's Vancouver store. Even though this action happened indoors, it can still be described as uncovered, inasmuch as GAP's idea was to create total havoc in its branch, including the hotdog stand and parking lot. It even had people walking around on their hands in front of the entrance![12]

EVENT ACTIONS

Event actions can take the form of a "happening" or a "flash mob"—a temporary mobilization of people around dancing, singing, or any games and competitions that are open to all.

To get people to talk about them, brands increasingly play with their public, trying to cajole fans into making some kind of contribution to the overall effort. It is something that brands, organizations, groups, associations, schools, and political parties all do. The aim is to get a large number of people to come together in one location and then tell everyone that this has happened. These kinds of operations, which were very popular between 2010 and 2012, can often be humorous as well. They allow companies to show themselves in a sympathetic and human light, with a slightly underground and funny image. One example from 2012 saw the cereal brand Kellogg's organizing France's biggest-ever lunch in the town of Charenton-le-Pont, with 450 people breakfasting for free while wearing the brand's colors.[13]

STREET MARKETING AND CONNECTED OBJECTS

Recent years have seen the emergence of new forms of alternative communication. Companies now rely on connected tools, surprising their audiences with unconventional campaigns (Street Marketing™, guerrilla marketing, and buzz), seeking an optimal dose of impact and technological prowess—even where this means their campaigns lose in creativity.

British Airways, for instance, had a billboard at Piccadilly Circus in London where every time a plane flew overhead, the child portrayed on the digital panel would look up in wonderment and point to the plane in the sky. In a market where consumers see six thousand advertising messages a month, it is capital for companies to show as much creativity as possible, to lock in existing customers and attract new ones. With the advent of connected objects and increasingly innovative technologies, Street Marketing has many clever new weapons at its disposal. Companies use these tools to differentiate themselves—but also in a way that turns the traditional rules of alternative marketing upside down. In an approach originally defined by creativity and inexpensive street innovations, companies today are starting to invest more in technology. To some extent, this signals the return of unconventional marketing.

Electronic Animation as the Seventh Dimension of Street Marketing

Until recently, street marketing was considered to comprise six main dimensions: the distribution of flyers; product operations; human operations; uncovered actions; event actions; and road shows. At a time when the digital world is conquering all before it, a seventh dimension seems to have arrived, one that is further upsetting the applecart of established codes. This is electronic animation, a new face of street marketing, characterized by electronic tools that use augmented reality to reshape urban furniture, creating new spaces where brands can express themselves. Pepsi Max, for instance, has developed an innovative electronic animation customizing a London bus stop, with each side of the structure serving as a see-through screen and using augmented reality to show an extra-terrestrial invasion, a tiger, or giant tentacles coming out of the ground. In this way, Pepsi Max is helping Londoners to experience a moment that they are not close to forgetting, mixing interactions and animations of the highest quality.

Technology at the Service of Street Marketing: A Winning Combination

The principle underlying electronic animation as an alternative method of communication is that people need to feel a "wow factor" as they go about their daily business. The effect of surprise can be very useful toward this end. The Swedish chain Apotek understood this very clearly with an innovative operation that it ran in the Stockholm subway to promote its latest range of shampoo. The company equipped a display panel with sensors to detect passing trains. Every time one came by, the hair would stand up on the head of the model shown on the panel. By so doing, Apotek could demonstrate how silky and light its shampoo makes users' hairs feel.

Street marketing is notably characterized by the way it uses the street to communicate inexpensively. The redeployment of urban furniture bolsters claims of street credibility and creativity, quanta that must be constantly recharged if marketers are to stay in tune with the authentic and non-institutionalized street codes that Generation Y consumers are so fond of. Street marketing has been responsible for some of this transition to a more digitalized universe. By so doing, however, it has lost some of its soul, including two original features that were so important to it for so long: street credibility and low cost. One example is the Tokyo Zoo, whose augmented reality street application lets people use their phones to follow virtual penguins leading them from the city's train station to the zoo.[14]

Street marketing itself is being reshaped. Technological progress might mean higher costs but also intensifies the impact on consumers. Brands are being publicized in innovative and cutting-edge ways. Costs may be higher than in traditional guerrilla marketing campaigns, but they are still lower than traditional media. This alters the definition of Street Marketing™.

The lesson for marketing specialists is not to depend too much on technological prowess to the point of ignoring the charms of the streets in which the technology is playing out. More than anything else, it is the street that connects an action to its locality.

Case in Point: Coca-Cola and Connected Street Marketing

In 2013 Coca-Cola wanted to undertake a communications effort enhancing the image and notoriety of its Coca-Cola Burn energy drink in France. Toward this end, the agency in charge of the operation (Game and Buzz Factory) proposed an innovative multi-channel operation taking advantage of Coca-Cola's partnerships with Lotus, the Formula One (F1) company, and Total City gas stations. The offbeat idea was to transform a purely functional location where users fill up their tanks into a street marketing experience that would be connected, fun, and engaging. The aim was to capture the heretofore neglected audience of gas station customers. Basically, the idea was to surprise drivers by promoting a well-known consumer brand.

Customers arriving at Total City's 1,030-strong networks of gas stations in France would discover—thanks to visual prints incorporating QR codes positioned at strategic points in the stations—that while filling up they could play a game where they would compare themselves with leading F1 drivers. This was particularly intriguing since the game incorporated participants' personal circumstances (geo-localization, behavioral triggers, etc.) To make it even more attractive, players were linked into the brand universe surrounding the sport, featuring items like F1 Lotus apparel and invitations to F1 events or races.

The operation was remarkably successful, with more than twenty million people being exposed to it for nearly a month at more than a thousand gas stations. Participants discovered Coca-Cola Burn and shared news about the operation through their social networks or by e-mail. Not only did the buzz develop in these networks, but the level of engagement exceeded expectations thanks to gamification's addictive mechanisms: some drivers would stay longer in the gas stations to give themselves a chance to beat the world's leading F1 drivers in the game.

This was a successful gamble for Coca-Cola, which has proved itself capable of engaging with people both offline (in the streets and via outdoor marketing) and online, helping the gas station sector to enter the digital world for the first time.

PRACTICAL STREET MARKETING RULES

Street marketing might assume a variety of different forms, but every one of them has a certain number of shared rules that they must respect. There is no doubt that street marketing operations can be challenging. This is particularly acute because professionals rarely take the pre-operational analytical phase as seriously as they should. The operations that end up running are not always the best ones, meaning they can have large opportunity costs. If an operation chooses a suboptimal location, for instance, it will obviously reach a smaller audience than it would have done otherwise.

These strategic analysis–related problems are not the only obstacles that companies face. Many problems come from the operational phase— when the operational actually happens. These problems often turn out to be very complex, between all the many steps that need to happen.

First, it is crucial that the operation take place at the specific location determined during the pre-campaign strategic analysis phase. Timing is also key, since the operation must happen at a time of the day when bystander numbers can be maximized.

Second, schedules must be respected. Given the temporary nature of a street marketing operation, everything has to be organized beforehand. During operationalization, all of the participants need to know their mission and get things done on time. This organizational competency is extremely important since it is the only guarantee that consumers will end up being surprised. Although many people might see an operation being set up (and understand what is coming), weakening the surprise effect can undermine future word-of-mouth. Hence the necessities of implementing the operation discreetly, so that when it happens, people are as surprised as possible.

Third, it is advisable to work with street marketing professionals when arranging an operation. They will be in a position to make proposals and provide advertisers with platforms meeting corporate objectives. The success of an operation is due, in part, to the quality of these platforms. It is hard to imagine that WWF would have had the same effect had people not seen its advertisement showing planet Earth covered in a dark balloon. By puncturing the balloon and revealing what lay below, the company successfully symbolized the pollution affecting modern civilization, heightening people's desire to do something about it.

Fourth, a street marketing operation must be visible and easily identifiable. This relates directly to the location chosen for its operationalization— but not only to this. In reality, there are two possibilities at this level.

Either the operation requires the participation of "street teamers" working to make the campaign more visible, or else its attractiveness depends on the platform itself and/or the operation's originality.

Finally, a street marketing operation can be either legal or illegal, as will be discussed further. This depends on whether authorization has been received from relevant national, municipal, or local authorities—or even the neighborhood organizations where the operation occurs. After all, an action can be declared illegal simply because it does not comply with the laws applying in the chosen location.

In sum, the rules to respect when preparing and carrying out street marketing operation involve choice of location; optimal timing; rigorous organization; high-quality, attractive, and realistic platforms; optimal visibility; and legal framework. Nor should anyone forget media complementarity, which must be done in parallel and before the operationalization.

WHERE MEDIA AND BUZZ COMPLEMENT ONE ANOTHER

Carrying out a street marketing operation is one thing. Optimizing the chances of high-quality word-of-mouth is another. It is worth remembering that the main objective of an alternative marketing campaign is to reach consumers in their daily lives, surprising them and getting noticed, so that they will want to share the experience through their networks. The problem with street market operations is that they all have one major limitation: namely, a limited geographic scope. However original they might be, they only touch direct spectators. To remedy this shortcoming, companies have no choice but to rely on broadcast media communicating their message on a wider scale. This explains why so many operations have been filmed to show how the campaign itself was managed, as well as the reactions of the people present. After being edited and finalized, these videos then go online, either through social networks or using wider broadcasting platforms such as YouTube or DailyMotion.

The only thing enabling these messages to be disseminated quickly and extensively is a digital platform open to all. The most original, creative, and impactful videos are generally viewed most often online. Advertisers and agencies are well aware of the importance of regularly monitoring that social networks are disseminating their bigger operations, notably to track the changing roles of the consumers following them as they evolve from simple observers to protagonists spreading word-of-mouth about an operation.

There are numerous examples of companies that have succeeded in generating high-quality word-of-mouth following a street marketing campaign. One seminal example is Europcar's AutoLiberté, discussed earlier. Another involves an operation carried out by La Belle Chaurienne, a specialist cassoulet maker. With the help of its communications agency, this French company organized an operation that generated a great deal of buzz online. The premise was an English person in the French provincial town of Castelnaudary (the country's main cassoulet production region) saying that cassoulet is English, not French. Market shoppers, shocked by the statement, often had funny reactions. The video filmed during the operation was good enough to generate more than 850,000 views on YouTube.[15] The Languedoc Conserverie canning company that sells La Belle Chaurienne–brand goods broadcast the video on different platforms while also blogging about it.

WHERE STREET MARKETING GOES WRONG

To ensure that an unconventional marketing operation succeeds and does not create a bad buzz, certain excesses must be avoided. As aforementioned, street marketing tries to create a direct connection with consumers and generate word-of-mouth. This opportunity can on occasion be transformed into a threat, however. After all, if a street marketing operation does not work, spectators might widely disseminate a negative image of the company.

Operational Limitations

Street marketing operations have yet to be fully conceptualized: their scope is vague, and their similarities and differences with other unconventional approaches are not always well understood. Moreover, many of their advantages and limitations have yet to be specified. More specifically, the legality of some street marketing operations poses a real dilemma for agencies and advertisers who are supposed to advertise lawfully, respecting competition regulations, intellectual property, and consumer protection statutes. From direct marketing to online advertising, agencies and advertisers have learned to incorporate into their thinking legal guidance protecting consumers' private lives. These constraints are often very legalistic in nature, probably reflecting the way street marketing has taken root in most of the world's largest cities. The question then becomes how to develop effective street marketing actions without committing illegalities—and how to create temporary spaces without receiving prior authorization.

Today it is imperative to act lawfully and in accordance with legal principles. Indeed, the avoidance of illegality is one of the first rules of a successful operation—that is, of course, unless the company is willing to face the consequences of its illegal actions (something which is increasingly infrequent). According to many professionals, it can take up to three months to prepare a good operation, and even then things might go wrong. There is always a chance that the authorities will take some measure that undermines the campaign, or that it will be simply rendered irrelevant because of things happening in other operations. In 2002, for instance, two completely naked spectators tattooed with Vodafone logos interrupted a rugby match between New Zealand and Australia, streaking across the field before being arrested by the police. Grahame Maher, a senior manager at Vodafone, asked public forgiveness for his company having encouraged the two supporters to interrupt the game. He promised to pay nearly $30,000 to a sports-related non-profit organization.

A 2008 example involves the Austrian brand Red Bull receiving permission to market its products in France. The company then decided that it wanted to organize a parade of 145 Mini Cooper S cars bearing its brand colors on Paris's Champs-Élysées Boulevard. It had not requested permission, probably because it knew that French authorities would never have agreed. Instead, Red Bull simply tried its luck, risking large fines for disturbing the peace. In the end, the operation was successful. It caused huge traffic jams in some of Paris's main intersections, but the online word-of-mouth was impressive.

Table 8.1 recaps the main issues surrounding the development of street marketing operations—not only domestically but also internationally. With relatively saturated markets, companies are forced to search constantly for new and different methods of communicating with consumers to show their offerings and stand apart from the rest. This can be done legally or illegally. The concept of legality is very important because the choice made by the company using unconventional marketing reflects its organizational philosophy. This book has provided several examples of companies who have succumbed in recent years to the charms of marketing practices and approaches that are unconventional and trying to differentiate themselves, yet keeping the cost margins much lower than would be the case with conventional communication initiatives. Note that the word "marketing" sometimes overstates the role played by these practices, considering the approaches are mostly below and rarely above

Table 8.1   Issues Surrounding the Development of Street Marketing Operations

DO	DO NOT
Start pre-event to do whatever is necessary to receive appropriate authorizations.	Commit illegalities and simply pay the fines (costs might be too high for limited events).
Have a clear vision of objectives and use this to develop a coherent structure surrounding the event.	Ignore potential impact on the company's image, blaming things on bureaucratic slowness.
Give the authorities a clear explanation of what the event will involve.	Launch a street marketing campaign that has ambiguous overtones (with nuclear power plants, etc.).
Do a detailed analysis of legal boundaries to avoid provoking regulators.	Break the law because this means a higher level of performance.
Do a global cost/benefit analysis on the campaign (including potential fines).	Accept delinquent behavior as the price of making a big splash.
Get good risk management advice to ensure legality.	
Develop transparency and communications between agency and advertiser to better ascertain the street marketing campaign's "risks."	

the marketing mix of the communication component. Street marketing has been particularly more widespread among all the different unconventional marketing approaches, especially companies that follow social media platforms (such as viral marketing).[16]

Compared to viral or buzz marketing, the conceptualization of street marketing has not been very clear. The range on street marketing has been defined roughly; other unorthodox approaches are rarely taken into account; and street marketing's advantages mostly remain unidentified. In specific, street marketing campaigns elevate a statutory problem that is still under-reported among marketers and businesses. At the hindmost, marketing operations are faced to meet the regulatory obligations and the rights of intellectual property owners that are intended to preserve healthy competition and, above all, to protect consumers. With direct marketing (followed by Internet marketing), marketers/advertisers have acquired to incorporate into their thinking Federal Trade Commission (FTC) regulations, this body being the United States' leading privacy policy and enforcement agency, which serves to protect consumer privacy. With an evolution of street marketing campaigns in most big cities, advertisers/marketers are faced with entirely new concerns, such as whether they can develop a successful street marketing campaign without any violations of FTC rules.

To date, the research on street marketing offerings in this area has been very limited. Black and Nevill's (2009) article on fly-posting is one exception, tackling problems relating to the built-in illegality of this medium.[17] The study was limited in scope because fly-posting constitutes only one street marketing approach, and the evaluations were focused upon consumers rather than the practitioners who are most directly impacted by the legal ramifications of the practice.

Hence the usefulness of helping managers to envisage their street marketing operations in a way that enhances understanding of the associated legal difficulties. To position the practice of street marketing more clearly, it should both be considered in all feasible unconventional communication approaches, and also have its dimensions specified, particularly its transgressive aspects. What is needed, then, is a qualitative study among agency and advertiser company managers who have recently developed striking street marketing operations. The goal here would be to establish the opportunities and threats of such operations, as well as agency–advertiser relationship-related considerations. Investigating the legal and ethical issues associated with street marketing practices is one way to ensure a lasting presence to the basics of street marketing theory.

The next chapter will focus on how to manage problems endemic to unconventional and street marketing campaigns. The focus will be the main limitations faced by companies applying such techniques.

Chapter 9

Evaluating Risk

Street marketing operations strive to meet any combination of the following objectives: (1) communicate with a particular (and often moving) target in its everyday environment; (2) generate word-of-mouth around a product, brand, cause, or institution; and (3) create connections between brand and consumers through real-life participation in memorable experiences. The advantages of a street marketing campaign for a company reside essentially in the directness of engagement and actual contact with a target, however mobile this may be. Through the experience and the ephemeral feelings shared between the company and the target, advertisers and agencies generate a sense of intimacy that resonates beyond the encounter. This feeling of nearness lasts longer insofar as the individuals affected can relive the encounter online and via social media. Generation Y, which broadly consists of young urbanites between the ages of fifteen and thirty, is often seen as the most suitable target for street campaigns, due to its association with street culture.[1] Street marketing today is understood more as creativity found in streets, such as street art and street culture, and not merely mobilizing street space.[2]

The main components of street culture include hip-hop or rap music as well as forceful and positive styles of dress.[3] All of this dictates a great number of fashion trends in the modern world. Posters, stencils, stickers, painting, installations, mosaics, or street shows in populated or crowded spaces may comprise street art. Authorized or not, these artists share a common activity, and they are intervening in their cities. The transformation to the urban space, particularly the streets, may be temporary or permanent.

Street art constitutes a subversive activity, because it uses public space and invents expressions that are paradoxical and reformulated modes of communication, all of which in turn inform street marketing practices. For agencies and advertisers, street marketing comes with statutory risk and constraints for which they are not generally prepared.[4] The main problem is that street campaigns require the use of public space and therefore require authorization from government authorities to be legal in using the space specified. The authorization needs to be confirmed for everything from simple operations like distributing flyers to more complex operations like the mobilization of products or people, or indeed for disguised campaigns.

The authorizations needed to perform campaigns are often quite difficult to obtain, as the time between planning and realization is limited. For safety reasons, many potential operations have failed to obtain authorization, and it is even forbidden to undertake a street marketing campaign in certain urban areas. In those situations, many agencies and advertisers will simply do without authorization. The question then becomes how and on what basis such choices can be justified, based on their impact on operational performance and cost; and how the agency–advertiser relationship is transformed. All these questions are crucial to the development of street marketing operations today.

TRANSGRESSING STREET MARKETING OPERATIONAL RULES

A descriptive design study that appeared previously in the *Journal of Marketing Communications* can be useful in answering these questions. The study consisted of a set of long conversations with managers at five advertisers and ten agencies engaged in street marketing operations in the United States and Canada.[5] Investigators focused on the most successful street marketing operations, identified from two years previous, which had achieved strong viral impact (e.g., on Facebook, Google, or YouTube), and sought out the responsible agencies, designers, or advertisers. The conversations on average lasted for forty minutes, involving up to three persons per company.

Each interview started with a presentation by the managers of the company and its activities, followed by details of one failed and one successful street marketing operation. They moved on to focus on the study's specific topics: the agency's street operations; their illicit dimension;

performance figures without authorization; the costs of breaking regulations; and how the agency–advertiser relationship is affected by breaking the rules. Working together with advertisers and agencies, the interviews were subjected to an inter-textual thematic analysis. Another goal of this final stage was to isolate possible contradictions.

ADVERTISERS, AGENCIES, AND REGULATIONS

The major advertisers reported staying mostly within the confines of statutory frameworks. According to the marketing director of one transport company based in Toronto, "All campaigns have been run totally above-board with permits for street use, photographic equipment positioning, sample giveaway, and use of sidewalks for demonstrations." The lawfulness of street marketing is a non-negotiable point, as large advertisers cautiously avoid breaking rules out of concern for the brand's reputation. This point was developed by four main actors working for different companies out of Toronto, Atlanta, or Sunnyvale, California. As a matter of course, the companies involved always request and obtain requisite authorizations before pursuing street campaigns. This obliges them to carefully prepare their street marketing operations: "We began to work in January for the operations realized in May," affirmed the senior director of experiential marketing of an Internet platform company based in Sunnyvale. There are exceptions, however. For instance, the CEO of a music market company based in San Diego accepted that smaller companies might on occasion have good reason to break the rules: "We would have to weigh the risks with the rewards. If we thought we could manage the damage or we could get away with the action, we would probably do it."

In contrast to the predominantly legalistic positioning of advertisers, agencies were a lot more lax about the possibility of engaging in an operation without authorization. All agency managers, to a certain extent, admit that they have engaged in unlawful operations and/or tried to overlook the rules. At the same time, large internationally recognized advertising agencies differed to some extent from the unorthodox and street marketing agencies that were small and independent, with the later tending to be transgressive or very transgressive. There were exceptions to this pattern, however, with two of the smaller agencies being relatively compliant.

All in all, there seems to be no inherent propensity for a particular type of organization in terms of breaking the rules or not. Other factors, such as the internal culture (influenced by the agency's overheads), the history, the chosen strategy and positioning chosen, and the kinds of customers that the brand serves (or wants to start serving) must be taken into account. In the words of the creative director of a Toronto-based communications agency, "We never, honestly, do illegal street campaigns because of the risk to our customers. Our customers are very big."

Unauthorized campaign-developing agencies in urban spaces would openly acknowledge their transgressive activities:

- "I've never asked for authorizations, never! We don't really need them for the street I use. Otherwise the places for which I would ask for an authorization, they will never give me. I know I won't be able to go there and they will never accept." —President of a New York–based events agency
- "Guerrilla and street marketing are called non-permission–based; you don't have a permit in a public domain where you can possibly get in trouble." —CEO of a New York-based guerrilla communications agency
- "True guerrilla marketing campaigns are almost always illegal in one way or another, as in most cases we do not ask permission to do whatever it is we are doing. That is why it is called guerrilla marketing." —Owner of a Seattle-based ambient communications agency

On the whole, when it comes to respecting or breaking the rules in street marketing campaigns, large and international agencies and advertisers tend toward legality, while the smaller companies tend toward transgression. When examined separately, however, all reported either episodic or continuous infringements. Hence the importance of understanding how managers justify this choice.

DENYING RESPONSIBILITY

Transcripts of interviews with some advertisers and agency managers reveal an arsenal of techniques for removing illegality. By applying the criminological theory of neutralization[6] to deviant consumption, it becomes possible to underline some of these techniques that allow managers to dissociate themselves from their crimes[7] by denying responsibility and transferring it on to others:

- Responsibility denial in which the person cites the difficulty of obtaining authorization, plus the compulsion that ultimately originated with this difficulty. Thus, according to the president of a New York–based guerrilla communications agency, "Brands often go the guerrilla route when the concept would not be permitted by the city, they don't have enough time to secure city permits and/or they don't have enough money for the city permits."
- Condemnation of the fact that the persons responsible for applying the rules are themselves not above suspicion. "The representatives of certain cities will never authorize a street marketing event. But on the other hand they are

going to accept events such as festivals, for example." —Project manager at a New York–based guerrilla communication agency.

- Denial of victims and damages, with the manager asserting that no damage had been done and deferring to a "minimalist" approach to ethics, the essence of which was to avoid damage to others.[8] This was the subtext when interviewees disagreed that their actions were degrading public spaces, contrary to what local authorities were saying. A senior account director from a New York–based communications agency confirmed this point: "Often cities are afraid of degradation and vandalization of property." Advertisement managers even spoke of helping to improve their urbanity.

- Citation of higher authorities, with the manager disagreeing with the regulations. Essentially, certain managers offered a moral justification for their transgressive campaigns, deferring to a "maximalist" approach to ethics predicated on a fundamentally moral world.[9] In some small agencies, this could involve a justification of the economic order—for instance, a project manager at a New York–based guerrilla communications agency remarked, "The illegality is here mainly a question of obligation of the needs of a commercial activity, forced independently of any explicit will to act illegally; it is the difference with the turned out crime." It could involve an artistic justification, a claim formulated by agencies "born in the street," with some including referents such as "Urban" or "Street" in their company names—the focus here being to profess their affinity with street art and also to give the impression of being "pirate organizations."[10]

THE NEED FOR SUCCESSFUL ORGANIZATIONS TO BE TRANSGRESSIVE

A commonly accepted and discussed point of view is that even breaking rules only makes the operation possible but does not necessarily make street marketing campaigns more successful. However, for many actors, agencies as well as advertisers, the illicit dimension enhances the effectiveness of a campaign, particularly by increasing room to maneuver and especially because this generates word-of-mouth:

- "No, illegality is not necessary for the success of a campaign, while yes some will take more chances than others . . . by causing some offence they may generate more of a buzz and get more people talking about the brand." —CEO of a New York–based guerrilla communications agency

An interesting option for most formal actors is to feign transgression, thereby reaping its rewards without the associated inconvenience.

- "Regarding efficiency, we have some customers that will pay for permits, but we still make it in a way that will stay guerrilla marketing, meaning we pay to be there but are making as if it was a non-permission." —CEO of a New York–based guerrilla communications agency

Transgression grants "street cred" (short for "street credibility") to street marketing operations. The term comes from the world of hip-hop and denotes a non-institutional and authentic dimension that is very important to Generation Y consumers, as seen by urban culture agencies. Depending on the objective of the operation, other factors play important roles in the effectiveness of any street marketing operation, so we must not give importance only to transgression.

GETTING AUTHORIZATION COSTS MORE THAN BREAKING THE RULES

Depending on whether managers have chosen to respect the rules, a street marketing campaign can be calculated in two different ways. In the first case, the cost of authorizations for a lawful operation dominates; such authorizations need to be obtained in advance. These costs can be intimidating even to the most legalistic, as may what they might consider the disproportionate efforts required to follow the rules:

- "Getting a permit to be in major city streets in for one day in the U.S. can be $10,000 to $100,000." —CEO of New York–based guerrilla communications agency

Otherwise, the only way to know the real cost of an illicit operation is to learn after it happens, on the basis of whether any penalties are charged:

- "If there is a breach and police are notified then yes a ticket and fine should be issued depending on the severity of the breach then yes a trial and more severe actions should be taken." —Marketing coordinator of Toronto-based transport company

For agencies that are prone to transgressing, scenarios are fraught with anticipation.

- "The most important thing is to know the consequences and liabilities of your actions. Make sure you bill enough to cover all potential risk so if anything does go wrong you are prepared. Make sure you have good legal standing by, in case you need them. The fact is, you will need legal from time to time, but if you do your research and homework well in advance of executing then you should know what you are getting into and the potential pitfalls. Plan for all potential scenarios." —Owner, Seattle-based ambient communications agency

THE ADVERTISER–AGENCY RELATIONSHIP AND THE RISKS OF TRANSGRESSION

The relationship between agency and advertiser turns on a simple principle: as a last resort, the advertiser will bear the consequences of the decision to initiate a non-compliant campaign, and the agency will be proactive on statutory questions, making only proposals while informing its counterpart of potential risks.

- "For our part as a communication agency, we have the obligation to inform our customers of the risks incurred in case of problems with law enforcement." —Senior accountant director of New York–based communications agency
- "When an operation of street marketing is proposed to a customer, we indicate to him the authorizations necessary to obtain so that everything takes place within the rules. It is then up to him to decide if he wishes to take the risk or not to break rules and to be penalized." —Project manager of New York–based guerrilla communications agency

Agencies are nevertheless cited by the advertisers as frequently being too proactive in proposing illicit operations:

- "Fines can be paid, but the worst costs to manage are the negative impact to brand reputation, and, potentially, if any activity leads to putting human life in danger." —Senior Director of experiential marketing at Sunnyvale-based Internet platform company

The courage to "speak wild" about using illicit communication approaches has been noted in few brands that are established, according to the agencies (c.f. president of a New York–based events agency). Most agency customers are small brands targeting young consumer audiences. Certain agencies may take steps to break rules and take the risk factor themselves when an advertiser lacks the courage to do:

- "Sometimes the advertisers know, but sometimes not. Later if there is a problem during the operation of street, the agency can be questioned as the advertiser, or both; but it depends on several parameters." —Owner of Seattle-based ambient communications agency

Thus when organizing a street marketing campaign, there could be some trust issues arising between the agencies and the advertisers, regarding whether to bend or break rules with some campaigns. The agency and advertisers' relationship can hang by a thread in delegating the penal risks and measuring the operations' ethical factors against expected results and profits.[11]

DECIDING ON A STREET MARKETING CAMPAIGN

To measure the managerial impression of the potential profits of a campaign, they must be considered in light of each company's specific context and the limits of the agency–advertiser relationship framework.

Being Transgressive

Street marketing campaigns may place organizations in a situation of breaking rules and regulations with unconventional methods of new media.[12] The organization, advertiser, or agency evaluating whether they should break rules must consider three dimensions:

1. Legal dimension: The legal risk factors invoved in the probability of being identified and the financial pentalties in both functions and the cost of authorization in scale of magnitude.

2. Economic dimension: The level of difficulty in organizing a campaign, the amount of money and time involved, word-of-mouth enhancement, and expected success rate among the target audience must be weighed against the interest in breaking the rules.

3. Ethical dimension: As subsumed in each organization's main justification logic or "orders of worth,"[13] which may be economic, artistic, ecological, etc.

The following section on U.S. regulations recaps these points. Breaking regulations does not always correlate with an unethical operation, at least for the actors. The justification is carried out in how the public perceive the campaign or operation. A campaign is considered ethical as long as the operations performed do not harm the public mentally or physically and do not hurt anyone's practices or beliefs. In some cases, a clearly unlawful operation could turn out to be ethical according to a particular moral vision. Hence, some environmentalist operations that use unorthodox techniques, or green marketing campaigns that use unconventional techniques to promote social or environmental causes,[14] are considered ethical despite often being unlawful. That said, Sony Ericsson's stealth marketing campaigns using phony tourists[15] is deemeed unethical and unlawful because they deliberately deceived consumers.

Professionals have even devised a grading scale in terms of how street marketing campaigns are received:

A: Any operation that is perceived as ethical and lawful
B: Unethical yet lawful
C: Unlawful but ethical
D: Unethical and unlawful

Getting around the Rules without Breaking Them

These findings raise questions about the way managers using unconventional communication tend to deny responsibility for their acts—and whether they are simply making excuses for their lack of preparation. Advertisers and agencies have shown that with a certain level of investment and very little planning, compliant operations are not only possible but can also be successful. Furthermore, many campaigns do not require government authorization yet offer all pros of a street campaign. Take, for instance, large organizations with showrooms and stores that do not require any authorization to perform a street marketing campaign at their doorstep.

To generate buzz, agencies have now turned their attention toward "reverse graffiti," due to the increase in the regulation of street graffiti and related practices (sometimes to the point of being prohibited). An American household cleaner brand, the Clorox Company, used "reverse graffiti operation" art called Green Works, where the entire operation was made from plants. For advertisers or agencies who do not wish to break the rules, while attaining the benefits and rewards of street marketing, these types of operations will open wide ranges of possibilities. As long as an organization stays within the limits of statutory framework, it is not a question of breaking the rules; the question then is only how effective the campaign is.

Managing Transgressions

The requirements of given situations such as place, targets, or objectives, may modulate the choice of breaking rules. The choice of breaking rules lies with the relationship between agency and advertiser and is rarely made in a vacuum, as the decision comes in jointly. Proactive agencies will have more chances of their offerings being accepted by advertisers, as they are capable of anticipating the needs that may break marketing practices.[16] As a priority, the advertisers will need something new and different from other agencies, to show their difference from the competition; therefore agencies attempt to surprise both advertisers and consumers with extreme propositions before they surprise the target audience. Essentially, advertisers urge agencies to innovate to help them differentiate.

If there is any breach, and if the backing company is identified, then the advertiser will be at major risk. Otherwise, the only other risk is collapse or breakdown in bringing the campaign to a successful completion (or, in the worst-case scenario, when law enforcement confiscates or destroys materials). The transgression therefore involves an attempt to create a healthy balance between future risk and probable gains. The risk aversion, however, has a limit, no matter how seriously the agency or advertisers take them into consideration.[17] It is crucial to finely specify and define all possible risks to attain an idea of risk management. Under this analysis, agencies may end up dropping out of the game, whether the analysis is done consciously or unconsciously. Indeed, when signing a contract on conducting a street marketing campaign with an organization or advertiser, agencies tend to come to terms by organizing a competitive procurement process, which sometimes turns out to be soft calls. To make the proposal more acceptable to their customers, agencies are trained to propose to advertisers what they want to hear. Therefore it is very sensible for the advertisers to have at least one person for legal advice, for questions and answers on legal aspects of any street marketing campaign.

As street marketing has become increasingly popular with companies, more specialized agencies are concentrating on it. This unorthodox means of communication creates stunning events that can help any company or brand to increase its profile, moving away from conventional means such as flyer distribution or pop-up stores. To promote communication, street marketing preserves the rules and codes of street art and street culture.[18] These kinds of street marketing activities are more attractive to young people living in urban areas; such activities are more likely to reach them, as they are not attracted to traditional communications, compared to past generations.

Street campaigns are challenging for advertisers, bringing to light a problem that has received scant attention to date. Even a temporary occupation of urban spaces is governed by very strict regulations precluding these campaigns' realization. Some actors choose to flout the regulations to succeed in their campaign. The decision takes into account the great potential financial gains, overlooking legal risk factors. To make an informed decision, marketing professionals must depend on legal skills that, ideally, should be integrated into their marketing departments.

The study in question has contributed to current debate about the ethics of guerrilla marketing campaigns based on the premise that "companies just cannot do anything because it works or can be done."[19] By focusing on how the advertiser–agency relationship affects the decision of whether short-term marketing ambitions justify breaking the law (or at least, the social contract), the study gives us a template for grasping and guiding the effectiveness underpinning this decision.

If companies using unconventional marketing campaigns want to avoid illegality, they can always try to get official authorization. There are models for this kind of approach.

Model Authorization for a Public Demonstration

Last name: _____

First name: _____

Address: _____

Title: _____

Tel.: _____

Fax: _____

Email: _____

Organizer Information

Date: _____

Timing: _____

Location: _____

Nature

Street marketing operation for Zélia, a designer brand.

Event Details

A young woman wearing a bridal dress started going through the streets of New York inside of a human-sized bubble draped with a ribbon displaying the Zélia brand. The operation began at 2 PM in Times Square and lasted 25 minutes (10 minutes for the setup and 15 minutes to carry it out). Called "Light as a feather," this was a street marketing operation that allied romanticism with modernity. Bystanders all stopped to look at the bride, as did retailers and tourists. Each was given a flyer. At the end of the operation, the groom arrived to pick up the bride in a chauffeur-driven car.

Expected number of spectators or participants: Between 150 and 250

Expected number of staff members (aside from security staff):

1 model playing the bride
1 model playing the groom
1 model playing the driver
2 persons in charge of logistics
3 guards
1 wardrobe specialist
1 makeup specialist
Total: 10 people

Refusing to Acknowledge an Operation's Delinquency[20]

Advertisers generally say that they will play by the rules, except in those few situations where getting the necessary authorization is almost impossible. Indeed, for some advertisers, it is inconceivable that they would run an illegal street operation. This might be for ethical reasons, due to their status as a public company or a cooperative—or simply because they want to protect their reputation. Great attention is paid here to the potential consequences of any street marketing operation before it gets started.

Illegality is first and foremost a position chosen by non-profit organizations seeking to change mindsets in any way possible, including by resorting to high-profile actions that might leave them open to lawsuits.

Unlike advertisers (most of whom take highly legalistic stances), agencies tend not to have a strict position toward unauthorized operations. Agency directors often admit that at some point they have carried out illegal operations and/or broken rules. Some agencies are quite open about this and speak in very specific terms, using guerrilla language to refer to their unauthorized actions, describing them as "wild" or "commando." A whole panoply of techniques are employed to downplay these illegalities. Advertisers and agency managers often deny responsibility, and/or deny that any damage has been caused. They also often refuse to recognize that anyone might be hurt by their actions, invoking higher criteria (such as the need to increase revenues) in a bid to turn the spotlight on their critics.

Operations That Succeed *Because* They Are Illegal

Illegality can facilitate the organization of street actions. To obtain the same outcome acting legally, organizers often need to embark upon a long and cumbersome process, which many advertisers do not want to do. On the other hand, there are also many players (both agencies and advertisers) for whom illegality is actually a way of increasing their performance and room to maneuver. Above all, it generates word-of-mouth.

One interesting option for the more legally-minded actors is to skirt illegality in a way that benefits from it without suffering any of the disadvantages. Illegality gives street marketing operations what hip-hop calls "street cred" (i.e., credibility). This is an authentic and noninstitutional dimension that is very popular among Generation Y consumers.

When Authorizations Cost More Than Infractions

There are two ways to calculate the cost of street marketing campaigns, based on whether the manager has been picked up for illegality or not. On the one hand is the cost of the requisite authorization. All advertisers, even the most legally minded, say this can be very high, making lawful actions disproportionately expensive. On the other hand, the real costs of a street marketing operation are only known afterward, depending on what fines have to be paid. For many agencies and advertisers, this cost is acceptable.

In some countries, like France, regulations are very restrictive. At the same time, some countries—again, including France—are quite tolerant of infractions. Given the general sense that breaking the law happens all the time and is almost inevitable with street marketing, the question becomes how to manage this risk.

One example of the advertiser–agency relationship at work is when the Ubi Ben agency covered the Paris Statue of Liberty in a Tony Parker T-shirt. Here the illegality was decided upon by the advertiser (Nike), which calculated that its own ethical judgment was at stake, and that it would bear any penal consequences resulting from this action. The agency simply suggested the idea and told the advertiser what risks it faced. Its involvement stopped there.

At the same time, legalistic advertisers often blame agencies for inciting them to go over the top and organize illegal street marketing operations. The fact that the penal risks associated with an action's illegality are borne by by the agency can cause tensions with the advertiser—as can the way in which the operation's expected benefits overshadow ethical considerations. The question becomes how each party reacts to regulations in a particular country where it conducts its street marketing operations. An American case study provides a good example of this.

U.S. REGULATIONS

A variety of rules can apply to street marketing operations, ranging from the simple distribution of flyers to the organization of relatively complex events.

Concerns about Street Marketing

As Bernard Cova has shown,[21] when it comes to outdoor marketing campaigns, business managers can be lax about legality. This is because it tends to be easier to ask for forgiveness than permission. Transgression costs are generally considered low and campaign benefits high. Having said that, some people have different perspectives.

In 2012, a man named Jeff Olson joined a crowd protesting outside of a Bank of America branch in San Diego. Using washable chalk, he wrote "No thanks, big banks" and "Shame on Bank of America" on the sidewalk,[22] before sketching an image depicting the bank as an octopus using its tentacles to grab cash.[23] Olson was said to have been a longtime advocate for locally run businesses, including credit unions, farmer's markets, and food outlets.[24] When San Diego's City Attorney brought criminal charges against Olson, Bank of America representatives said that he was soliciting business for a rival credit union, adding to his anti-bank slogans imprecations such as "Switch to credit unions."[25] The story was that Olson received $25 for every account that opened as a result of his action.[26] In other words, even as he was using the street to express ideas, he was allegedly deploying a covert street marketing campaign on behalf of a credit union that could both gain customers and cast a shadow over the Bank of America brand.[27] In one act, Olson became both a street marketer and a "brandalist."[28]

Olson was charged with thirteen counts of graffiti vandalism for his chalk sidewalk art.[29] If convicted, he faced thirteen years in prison and over $6,000 in fines. The prosecutor pursued the case all the way to trial after Olson rejected a plea deal. The terms of the plea would have required Olson to attend an eight-hour seminar from the Corrective Behavior Institute, pay Bank of America nearly $6,300 in restitution, waive all Fourth Amendment search and seizure rights, and surrender his driver's license for three years. In the end, the jury acquitted Olson after the media lambasted the city for squandering money on a case involving expressions written with water-soluble chalk.[30]

Despite its happy ending, the Olson case exemplifies the risks faced by anyone using street marketing techniques to promote a brand. While some hazards associated with these campaigns can be adequately planned for, others cannot. Olson's protest, which involved about $5 worth of chalk, would have incurred thousands of dollars in legal fees had he not been represented pro bono. Furthermore, he faced thousands of dollars in fines and over a decade in jail. In part, this was due to broad and randomly enforced laws such as Cal. Penal Code §594. A marketing professional might believe that street art with washable chalk is unlikely to be prosecuted, or may be punished with only a small fine. However, the Olson case demonstrates that this is not necessarily an accurate risk assessment.

In another instance of enforcement, a Texas-based advertiser tried to promote Mini Cooper by placing a hollow, fiberglass shell, visually identical to a Mini Cooper, on the side of a Houston building. To pedestrians, it seemed that a Mini Cooper had somehow parked on the side of the building. In this case, the gamble paid off. There was extensive media attention and subsequent buzz. After the city issued a stern warning for affixing an object without a building permit—threatening a fine between $500 and $1,000—the advertiser removed the car. In the meantime, the controversy spread through the blogosphere, featuring everywhere from advertising websites to local news stations. The consequences for this transgression were miniscule compared to the benefits for the dealership.

One can see that marketing professionals' tendency to ignore legal implications can have different kinds of impact. On one hand, a campaign can have penal consequences of $500 to $1000, with benefits far in excess of this penalty. On the other, a campaign can have a fairly modest benefit of $25 for each new user, yet create a risk of jail time and massive financial consequences for its organizers. It is surprising that a campaign featuring a car attached to a building would create far less uproar than chalk sidewalk art. Given the wide disparity in legal risks, lawyers find this whole situation complicated. There is a need to address street marketing's legal risks, specifically looking at the kinds of issues facing guerrilla marketing professionals, which their attorneys should consider when evaluating outdoor marketing campaigns.

In short, this is a bourgeoning area of law, yet one that has not undergone any major analysis. More importantly, nothing has been done to help legal professionals find ways of advising companies and agencies about street marketing. There are probably two reasons for this. First, the legal profession is not fully aware of the need to provide legal analysis for street marketing because it is a relatively new field; and second, there is a perception among the marketing community that bringing in lawyers is too costly, takes too long, and in the end may even undermine a campaign's credibility, in cases where illegality enhances the desired buzz.

In short, there is clearly some value in today's legal and academic communities to start envisioning street marketing as a new and important area of law that merits further consideration. One starting place for this effort might be to delve into existing legislation, for instance in the state of California, to explore how they gel with street marketing campaigns.

California Laws

A guerrilla marketing campaign can potentially come under a whole array of statutes. Some are familiar, like vandalism or graffiti, while others are more specific, like the failure to obey flybill regulations or affixing signs to building without permissoin. To fully understand the legal challenges that guerrilla marketing specialists face, it is useful to survey state laws (such as the right of publicity or privacy) as well as penal statutes—in addition to county and city codes, which include procedures for obtaining permits covering signage and building modifications, news racks and newsstands, public gatherings, exhibitions, the distribution of flyers, public solicitations, outdoor advertising, and banners.

The city of San Diego is used to demonstrate the wide range of legal issues at stake in these situations. Table 9.1 outlines the kinds of laws that might be invoked in relation to a typical street marketing campaign

Table 9.1   Potential Legal Issues Related to Street Marketing in California

	California
Vandalism - PC § 594	• (b)(1) If $400+ in damage: imprisonment up to one year and/or a fine up to $10,000; or if the damage exceeds $10,000, a fine up to $50,000 • (b)(2)(A) If less than $400 in damage, imprisonment up to one year and/or a fine up to $1,000 • (b)(2)(B) If less than $400 in damage but if Δ has a previous conviction under §§ 594, 594.3 (vandalism of a place of worship), 594.4, 640.5, 640.6, or 640.7, imprisonment up to 1 year and/or a fine up to $5,000
Vandalism with a Caustic or Noxious Chemical or Substance - PC 594.4	Imprisonment up to 1 year and/or: (b)(1) If $50,000+ in damage, a fine up to $50,000 (b)(2) If $5,000–50,000 in damage, a fine up to $10,000 (b)(3) If $950–5,000 in damage, a fine up to $5,000 (b)(4) If less than $950 in damage, a fine up to $1,000
Graffiti on a Governmental Building or Vehicle - PC 640.5	(a) If $250 or less in damage, fine up to $1,000 and 48–200 hours of community service, or graffiti abatement (e.g., keep a specified area free of graffiti for 90 days) (b) If previous conviction under §§ 594, 594.3, 594.4, 640.5, 640.6 or 640.7: imprisonment up to 6 months and/or a fine up to $2,000 plus 96–400 hours of community service or graffiti abatement for 180 days (c) If two previous convictions under §§ 594, 594.3, 594.4, 640.5, 640.6, or 640.7: imprisonment up to one year and/or a fine up to $3,000 plus up to 600 hours of community service or 240 days of graffiti abatement (d) (1) In addition to the above-listed punishments, the Court may require Δ to perform the necessary labor to clean, repair, or replace the damaged property

Table 9.1 (*Continued*)

Graffiti of Private Property - PC 640.6	(a) If less than $250 in damage: a fine up to $1,000 and 48–200 hours of community service or 90 days of graffiti abatement (b) If previous conviction under §§ 594, 594.3, 594.4, 640.5, 640.6, or 640.7: imprisonment up to 6 months and/or a fine up to $2,000 plus 96–400 hours of community service or 180 days of graffiti abatement (c) If two previous convictions under §§ 594, 594.3, 594.4, 640.5, 640.6, or 640.7: imprisonment up to 1 year and/or a fine up to $3,000 plus up to 600 hours of community service or 240 days of graffiti abatement (d) In addition to the above-listed punishments, the Court may order Δ to perform the labor to clean, repair, or replace the property
Graffiti or Vandalism within 100 feet of a highway - PC 640.7	• 1st Offense: imprisonment up to 6 months and/or a fine up to $1,000 • 2nd Offense: imprisonment up to 1 year and/or a fine up to $1,000
Right of Publicity - Civ. Code § 3344	(a) Actual Damages or $750 per incident and any profits that are attributable to the unauthorized use that are not taken into account when determining actual damages
Physical Invasion of Privacy - PC 1708.8	(a) Knowingly entering onto private property without permission with intent to capture a visual image, sound recording, or other physical impression of a person (b) Constructive Invasion: attempting to capture, in a manner that is offensive to a reasonable person, any visual image, sound recording, or other physical impression when the plaintiff has a reasonable expectation of privacy (d) Damages up to three times any general and special damages proximately caused by the violation; if done for a commercial purpose, also subject to disgorgement of any proceeds or consideration obtained as a result of the violation, as well as a civil fine of $5,000–50,000 (e) Solicitation of a violation: liable for general, special and consequential damages, punitive damages, and a civil fine between $5,000-50,000
Trespass - PC 602	Imprisonment up to 6 months and/or a $1,000 fine
Unlawful Commercial Email Advertisements (Under Certain Conditions) - B&P § 17529 - 17529.9	17529.5/17529.8: Punishable by actual damages or liquidated damages up to $1,000 per each unsolicited commercial email with a maximum of $1,000,000 per incident; plus attorney's fees and costs

(Continued)

Table 9.1 (*Continued*)

Contribute to Delinquency of a Minor - PC 272	Imprisonment up to one year and/or a fine up to $2,500 and/or five years of probation
Littering Upon Public / Private Property - PC 374.4	1st Offense: mandatory fine between $250–1,000 2nd Offense: mandatory fine between $500–1,500 3+ Offenses: mandatory fine between $750–3,000 *In addition, court may require the person/corporation to pick up litter for 8+ hours
Prevent, Hinder, or Obstruct Access to or Egress from Property - PC 420.1	A fine up to $500
Disturbing a Public Meeting or Assembly - PC 403	Imprisonment up to 6 months or probation
Unlawful Assembly - PC 408	Imprisonment up to 6 months or probation
Refusal to Disperse at a Place of Riot or Unlawful Assembly - PC 409	Imprisonment up to 6 months or probation
Disturbing the Peace - PC 415	Imprisonment up to 90 days and/or a fine up to $400
Refusal to Disperse After Committing an Unlawful Act - PC 416	Imprisonment up to 6 months or probation
Public Nuisance - PC 372	$495

Where Authorization Seems Costlier Than Transgression

Marketing professoinals and business managers tend to believe that the cost of a street marketing operation can be calculated in two different ways depending on whether the managers have opted to respect the rules or not. In the first case, the cost of a lawful street operation largely depends on the cost of obtaining authorization in advance. On this subject, even the most legally-minded advertisers are clearly intimidated by the cost. In their view, efforts to remain within the rules are disproportionate: the perception is that obtaining a permit for one day in a major US city street can cost anywhere from $10,000 to $100,000.[31] Most permits cost only a few hundred dollars, but they require the use of specific, complicated forms, hence expensive attorneys. Further, participants in most marketing campaigns cannot anticipate all of the laws that might be broken. In this case, trying to comply can feel like an expensive goose chase. Ultimately, even a vetted campaign could violate some unforeseen law or be penalized arbitrarily using an obscure local code.

The second cost analysis option is to simply evaluate the potential cost of transgression, discounting that cost by the odds of enforcement. In other words,

$$\text{Risk of an Illegal Act} = (\text{probability of being caught}) \times (\text{sanction in terms of \$})$$

In order to assess risk, legal professionals must evaluate which regulations are most likely to be transgressed under federal, state, and local laws. Table 9.1 shows the laws that can be referred to when evaluating a campaign in San Diego.

Business and Legal Analysis

Street marketing's legal aspects do not appear to have been addressed yet in legal publications. Based on responses to research conducted by Cova and Saucet, managers of businesses clearly avoid addressing legal issues head-on and instead choose to conduct most campaigns without regard for legalities. In this regard, marketing professionals and businesses are neither undertaking the cost of compliance nor evaluating the cost/benefit of transgression. Presumably, the different parties should be able to make a more deliberate cost/benefit analysis about whether to ask permission or beg forgiveness. Legal professionals can provide tools and analysis to improve decision-making and lower the cost of compliance. Having said that, there is no golden book covering the legal issues involved here. Many of the legal issues associated with street marketing come from a plethora of local codes, cases, and statutes that might be interpreted differently at the municipal, county, state, and federal levels. It is doubtful that a law firm exists in the United States with "street marketing" listed as a specialty on its website. And yet this is a rapidly growing area of business practice that demands the attention of the legal community.

Many barriers prevent marketing specialists and managers from complying with different laws. For example, a permit fee may only be $30 and require just one form—but this form can be hard to find, or planning and compliance costs can create obstacles that people want to avoid. Furthermore, the authorizations required for many approvals may not be quick enough for a particular operation's timeframe. In such situations, many advertisers and agencies will simply launch the campaign, acting without any authorization.

All in all, three primary approaches are available to companies:

1. Ignoring legal issues entirely.
2. Using transgression as a business tool.
3. Following the rules and avoiding violating the law.

Ignoring Legal Issues Entirely

Interviews with managers at some advertisers and agencies reveal that various techniques exist for eschewing illegality.[32] The relevance of applying the criminological theory of neutralization[33] to deviant consumption highlights the fact that these managers use known techniques to remove themselves from their illegality and transfer responsibility to others:[34]

- "Blame-Shifting: Condemnation of the fact that the persons responsible for applying the rules are themselves not above suspicion.
- Denial of responsibility: The person cites the difficulty of obtaining authorization and a compulsion stemming from this: management of the time required to request authorization as well as the associated process.
- Denial of damages and victims: The manager asserts that no damage has been done and pursues a 'minimalist' approach to ethics, the essence of which is to avoid damaging others.[35]
- Input from higher authorities: The manager disagrees with regulations, offering a moral justification for the campaigns and pursues a 'maximalist' approach to ethics predicated on the existence of fundamentally moral world.[36] Justifications at this level can be economic in nature—but also of an artistic order where agencies 'born in the street' are involved (companies that use referents such as Urban or Street in their names and which claim an intimacy with street art to give the impression of being 'pirate organizations')."[37]

Many marketing professionals feel that ignoring legal issues makes campaigns easier to organize, even where illegality is unlikely to be a key issue. At the same time, for many parties (including agencies and advertisers), this illicit dimension is believed to enhance the effectiveness of a campaign. Illegality is seen as a way of generating buzz and free press, even if this relates to how the action's protagnonists have been sanctioned for violating laws through their street marketing campaign. The campaign's street credibility (a badge of authenticity) is also seen as being linked to its rebellious nature and rejection of modern business and political constraints—all qualities to which members of Generation X and Y are very sensitive. Of course, as mentioned earlier, depending on an operation's objectives, other factors will also be important for a street marketing campaign's effectiveness.

Typically, when conducting a risk/benefit analysis, an operation's illegality is of paramount concern. An illegal operation can result in criminal, civil, and administrative penalties that could damage (if not destroy) an organization's finances and credibility. Somewhat atypically, the illegality of a street marketing operation often creates unforeseen benefits. Similar to related areas of new and unconventional media communications,[38] street marketing operations place organizations in situations where breaking regulations may be inevitable, and in some cases desirable. As briefly touched upon above, organizations should contemplate the following three dimensions[39] when coming to a conclusion in breaking rules or not:

1. Lawfulness. This first factor can be quite complex. The calculation of legal risks includes the probability of prosecution, any associated penalties, and—conversely—the cost of authorizations, itself reflecting the licensing involved in permitting (and in some cases facilitating) private contracts. None of these factors are particularly simple. One example is flyers placed under car windshield wipers. There is a good chance that their distribution was not properly authorized. The question then becomes whether the relevant laws are ever enforced. This appears to be unlikely, meaning that the probability of prosecution is low. Yet if the authorities want to make an example out of someone, that person or group could be on the hook for hundreds of dollars for each flyer distributed, depending on the city. In a small marketing campaign, this could mean liabilities totaling several thousand dollars. Similarly, these offenses could be punished with administrative penalties—although the authorities do have the discretion to seek civil remedies, with any incidental damage that the campaign causes to private property potentially resulting in an independent legal action. On the other hand, it is hard to determine how much it costs to conduct a campaign legally. Many different licenses and permits are potentially applicable to every street marketing campaign. Negotiating with private property owners can be expensive, frustrating, and above all, unpredictable.

2. Economics. In addition to the costs associated with illegality, organizations must consider the long- and short-term benefits of street marketing. Like all advertising, the goal of street marketing is to create hype and make people talk about the brand or the product. Unlike traditional media advertising, street marketing typically has low organization and implementation costs, even though the value of exposure—especially where unique target markets are concerned—can be immense. In 2008, Zoo York, a streetwear company based in New York, captured hundreds of cockroaches and spraypainted on their backs the company logo, a variation of the letters "Z" and "Y." In a YouTube video viewed nearly 200,000 times, young men on skateboards and bicycles throw

the painted roaches at the well-dressed, prim pedestrians of Wall Street. This campaign may be repulsive to some, but to skateboarders, disaffected youths, and most importantly, the customers of Zoo York, it was truly awesome. The campaign likely produced massive value for the brand, for a very small price.

3. Ethics. A final consideration when deciding whether to pursue a potentially illegal campaign is the ethical message underpinning the advertisement. These justifications or orders of worth[40] may outweigh basic economic concerns. If the message is particularly ethical—for instance, a campaign by Nicorette advocating smoking cessation—the organization might come to the opinion that any illegality will be overshadowed by the benevolence it is manifesting. This recalls the previous discussion about the difference between asking permission and begging forgiveness. Human interest may be intangible and immeasurable, but it still has a role to play in risk/benefit analyses. If a product saves lives, an advertiser subject to sanctions is likelier to be shown greater mercy than if the product being sold is something like alcohol or tobacco. Ditto when street marketing is used to convey a "green" message, rather than merely promoting a product or service.

Using Transgression as a Business Tool

Street marketing campaigns are frequently undertaken in the absence of any assessment of risk. As aforementioned, the fact that street marketing can involve such a broad spectrum of legal issues means that the legal community is not well equipped to make efficient assessments of the legal risks that agencies or advertisers face. Hence the conclusion that the legal profession has not yet coalesced around street marketing. There are no tools; no seminal treatises; no experts capable of providing quick and effective answers to the questions that street marketing raises. Given the industry's growth, the time may be ripe for a body of "street marketing law" that experts can draw from to advise companies and advertising agencies.

It is clear that legal practitioners should be involved in analyzing the costs and benefits of complying with rules or breaking them. If a campaign does not produce a benefit far greater than the cost of compliance, the operator may choose to transgress. This is especially true where the product targets a younger, more rebellious generation going through a stage of rebellion against authority.

Following the Rules

Cova and Saucet's findings raise questions about the way managers using unconventional communication tend to deny responsibility for their acts—and whether they are simply making excuses. Agencies and brands or companies have shown that with certain amounts of investment, operation compliance and very little planning are not only possible but can also be successful. Furthermore, many campaigns do not require government authorization yet offer the credits of street marketing operation. For instance, large organizations with showrooms and stores do not require any authorization to perform a street marketing campaign at their doorstep. Indeed, in front of a store is a perfect place for carrying out lawful street operations.

Another example can be seen, where companies turn street marketing practices on their head. As regulation of street graffiti and related practices have increased (sometimes to the point of being prohibited), agencies have turned to "reverse graffiti" initiatives to generate buzz. The Clorox Company, an American household cleaner brand, launched its new product line called Green Works, made entirely from plants, with an accompanying art program entitled "the Reverse Graffiti Project." The project involved a pioneering graffiti artist using his medium to "clean" the wall of San Francisco's 140-meter-long Broadway Tunnel. This type of operation opens up a range of possibilities for those who do not want to break the rules, while retaining the advantages of street campaigns. It is not a question of breaking rules but bypassing them as far as possible while staying within the limits of the current statutory framework.

Another example is a street marketing campaign that was recently organized in conjunction with the United Nations World Council of Peoples. The goal was for a group of law students to create a hypothetical campaign and then analyze its legality for a "real" customer.

METHODOLOGY AND ANALYSIS

The World Council of People at the United Nations (WCPUN) functions on several levels when funding different projects worldwide, including the publication of a magazine called *Centerpoint Now*. One such project involved promoting a sustainable use of water resources. The street marketing campaign created toward this end made use of a public fountain and other features of public space. A videographer was hired to film the reactions of people passing by.

The campaign's legality was studied in both Los Angeles and New York City, using data source triangulation as a case study methodology.[41] In other words, a case study was built using two examples of guerrilla marketing street operations (see below, Guerrilla Marketing Ideas at the Street Level: Dirty Water Fountain). The legal issues pertaining to these two operations were then compared. In general, non-governmental organizations (NGOs) seek marketing opportunities that cost little. NGOs' use of street marketing can be all the more effective because of the way that street marketing provides access to people coming face-to-face with the NGO's message.

Case studies are often used in business and marketing analysis. Here we will use them as a means of evaluating the legal issues associated with street marketing.

GUERRILLA MARKETING IDEAS AT THE STREET LEVEL: DIRTY WATER FOUNTAIN

This street campaign appropriated a water fountain in one of New York's many public spaces. It dirtied the water by filling the fountain with dead fish and trash. It also had people lying around the fountain, supposedly dying of thirst.

Type of Operation:
Street/Viral Marketing

Pitch:
You are walking in New York, approaching a familiar plaza where a crowd has gathered. Everyone is looking at something. As you make your way through the crowd, you see brown water spraying high into the sky above everyone's heads. You make your way to the front and see a fountain (e.g., City Hall Park, Lincoln Center, Radio City Music Hall). The water is brownish black, full of dead fish floating on the surface. Emaciated people lie on the ground nearby, apparently dying of thirst.

You gasp at the scene and notice a sign: "Millions of people around the world drink water like this every day. *Centerpoint Now.*" A camera crew records the crowd's reactions. They approach you with a release. You sign in exchange for a copy of *Centerpoint Now.*

A few weeks later, a friend from high school sends you a Facebook message. She saw you on a YouTube video with thousands of hits. "Do people really drink water like that?" she asks.

"Yes," you reply. "Check out the article on clean water projects in *Centerpoint Now.*"

Operation's Relevance:
WCPUN participates in sustainable development projects, but the main purpose of the organization is to facilitate conversations within its network of luminaries. The *Centerpoint Now* magazine is authored by well-known public figures but has fairly limited distribution. The

Table 9.2 Potential Penalties of Not Obtaining a License or Permission

License(s)	Licensing Cost	Potential Violations if Done Without Permit/ License	Penalties
Private Use Permit/License	Negotiable	• Vandalism • Public nuisance • Littering • Unlawful distribution of hand-bills	
Release from People in the Video	Low (T-shirt, magazine, as nominal consideration)	• Right of publicity • False endorsement	Civil: could result in statutory amounts (i.e., $500 for Right of Publicity) or disgorgement of profits
Use of public fountain	$0	$0	No known penalties
Public gathering	$0	$0	No penalty for gathering under 20 people

recommendation was for WCPUN to find ways to take its message to the broader public, not just its existing network of members—the idea being that if the organization wants to be sustainable, it needs to invite greater participation from a wider audience.

Predicted Impact:

The promotion was projected to have different impacts at different points in time. Firstly, it would generate an immediate buzz in New York as people who experienced the promotion talked about it to their friends, families, and coworkers. Then, photos and videos taken by amateurs and local news stations would hit the Internet and local TV, generating a second buzz. This would be followed by the WCPUN releasing a professionally edited short video showing the reactions of bystanders at the fountain. All of this would be promoted online both through the WCPUN and the *Centerpoint Now* websites, and on social networks such as Facebook, Twitter, and Reddit. The long-term success of this operation would depend on WCPUN's ability to reinvent itself online.

Prerequisites:

1. Obtain a permit, where required, from the relevant authorities.
2. Contract a professional service to record, edit and secure releases from bystanders.

3. Rent barricades to prevent bystanders from going into the water.

4. Purchase large signs featuring the desired message.

Legal Difference between Los Angeles and New York

The students researched the legality of the campaign. It turned out that in New York, free use of the fountain was permitted, provided a courtesy call was made to the local police precinct, fewer than twenty people were involved, and no sound amplifiers were used. Assuming that any filmed pedestrians signed releases, the campaign could therefore be carried out in New York without violating any laws or any permits having to be obtained.

In Los Angeles, a permit would be required to use the fountain; another permit to film; and possibly a third permit to cover the people gathering. An NGO in this situation might therefore find that regulatory compliance in Los Angeles is unduly burdensome and either choose not to operate the campaign there or simply do it and risk the costs of the transgression.

In short, street marketing professionals would be happy with the cost of compliance in New York: low cost; no lead time; no formal obstacles; little risk of transgression or penalties. In Los Angeles, on the other hand,

Table 9.3   The Costs of Compliance in Los Angeles

License(s)	Licensing Cost	Administrative Penalty	Criminal Law	Civil Law
Building or Encroachment Permit (Cty. §§ 51.104 & 51.105)	If it qualifies as a "wall sign," $675	Double the amount of the permit fee	Erecting a sign without a building permit	• Cost of repairs/ abatement • Punitive Damages (unlikely)
Permission from Property Owner	Negotiable	N/A	• Unlawful handbill distribution • Vandalism • Graffiti	Abatement
Film Permit				
Public Gathering				
Permit to use public fountain				

it might seem more attractive to run the campaign and risk the penalties. With a little bit of lawyering, the cost of compliance can be calculated in various jurisdictions, providing customers with a way of weighing the cost/benefit of each jurisdiction. To repeat, however, it does appear that the legal profession is currently ill-equipped to provide customers with effective advice about street marketing campaigns.

Analyzing the Legalities of a Street Marketing Campaign

The purpose of this case study was originally to develop a matrix that a marketing campaign could use for simple evaluations. Research turns up hundreds of relevant codes and regulations in each city in California alone. In other words, there are hundreds of possible codes that can be used to evaluate the legality of a campaign in four Californian cities. A street marketing operation in a typical city might run up against municipal codes relating to signage, building permits, public gatherings, vandalism, the distribution of flyers, and many other local ordinances. The county will have regulations covering some of these same areas, especially where health issues are at stake. Then, on top of these city and county statutes there will be state codes, relating notably to vandalism and graffiti, rights of privacy and publicity, trespass, littering, assembly, disturbing the peace, and public nuisance. Lastly, the federal level offers defenses to certain basic rights like free speech—with other federal laws being more specific, relating to concerns like trademark and copyright law.

Marketing specialists, their customers, and legal professionals must all start taking these issues on board much more directly. It would seem that companies and agencies' current modus operandi makes this difficult, however. But instead of ignoring legal issues or breaking the law, a better starting point might be to ask legal questions. Businesses and marketing specialists often have an inaccurate perception that the cost of compliance is too high. A street marketing campaign need not cost $10,000 to $100,000 to operate legally. As demonstrated in the aforementioned "dirty water" case study, the cost can be virtually nonexistent. Given that each city and state has its own laws, however, it is impossible to say that a campaign with no risk in New York is also without risks in Los Angeles. Instead of this, the much better idea is to ask the same questions in both cities. As legal professionals begin to do this—and as more participants in the process opt for compliance instead of transgression—the cost of compliance will drop, to such an extent that marketing professionals will not be so afraid of it.

Research Limitations

The point to be made at this juncture is that the growth in street marketing is not likely to dissipate any time soon. Current participants are largely either ignoring the law or managing their transgressions. The legal community has not yet coalesced around street marketing in such a way as to provide methods of analysis that will help businesses and marketing specialists to make better decisions about street marketing legalities. A public debate must be started, one that will hopefully see the legal community start to devise street marketing solutions. It is at this level that recommendations should start, not in a book such as the present one, whose only advice should be that people must act legally and not violate any laws. The problem is that relevant laws are hard to find, sometimes costly to comply with, time-consuming. Moreover, in many cases they go unenforced. Yet it is still paramount that the relevant laws be uncovered, the means of compliance identified, and the business community provided with a means of compliance.

Right now, a marketing specialist working in Dallas cannot easily determine what laws might be violated by a street marketing campaign run in that city. The same applies in San Diego, Los Angeles, New York, Chicago, and every other city in the United States. The great hope is to see the drafting of seminal treatises and guidelines helping marketing specialists and their customers to improve their risk analysis, by complying with the law wherever possible, or else by choosing to manage their transgressions as best as possible where they have determined that the rewards outweigh the risks.

The concept of guerrilla marketing is something that many seem to view as inherently illegal. Street marketing is an unconventional communication activity. However, unconventional does not mean illegal. Once limited to basics such as sandwich men and the distribution of flyers, guerrilla marketing now covers a broad spectrum of activities: event actions, happenings, flashmobs, road shows, and many other means of generating an inexpensive buzz. These activities are becoming compulsory for companies. The question that remains is how to weigh the legal risks against often great economic opportunities.

NEGATIVE WORD-OF-MOUTH: HOW ILLEGALITY HARMED RENTABILIWEB

Rentabiliweb is a Belgian holding company with operations in Canada, Europe, and Asia. It specializes in monetizing audiences and is famous for developing the first single site offering profitable solutions to

Internet professionals.[42] Based on the principles of dedicated emailing, Rentabiliweb would portray its Mailorama.fr subsidiary as a platform performing much better than traditional direct marketing tools (and generating higher returns).

In November 2009, Rentabiliweb started a street marketing operation that became a catastrophy. The company had announced on its website that it was going to hand out nearly €40,000 to consumers in the street. Around 7,000 people waited for the operation to begin in Paris's Champ-de-Mars public space, right next to the Eiffel Tower. Given the size of the crowd, the organizers had to cancel the operation, causing a violent reaction from some people, who began vandalizing cars, throwing things at the police, and beating up photographers. Around a dozen arrests had to be made. One consquence was France's Minister for the Interior deciding to sue the event organizers despite their having received a formal authorization for the operation. The organizers defended themselves—in vain—by saying that the necessary security measures had been taken.

Clearly, the company was responsible for this chaotic situation, and it had to explain its operations to the police and other authorities in Paris. At the same time, word-of-mouth materialized very quickly, with many media outlets talking about how things had gone wrong. The fact that the publicity was viral had the effect of emphasizing the operation's negative sides, with the company being blamed for not having foreseen the consequences of its actions, as well as for its poor security management. Given the economic difficulties many people face at present, Rentabiliweb should have realized that this kind of operation would attract a huge crowd, which would include troublemakers. The company underestimated its action's attractiveness and did not hire enough security staff—something that might have improved the operation's organization and, above all, outcomes.

This example shows that word-of-mouth can be as much a threat as an opportunity. The truth is that street marketing requires real competency. Operations are serious, and any company that takes them lightly risks devastating consequences.

KEY POINTS IN PART 3—STREET MARKETING

1. All low-budget creative operations (aside from billboards and outdoor marketing) can be construed as street marketing.
2. All kinds of players resort to street marketing, ranging from cars to perfumes.
3. Guerrilla marketing practices vary from one country to the next but apply in some way or the other worldwide.
4. Campaigns start with a theoretical phase (benchmarking, strategic thinking, brainstorming) before moving on to operations when the strategy will be applied.
5. Budgets tend to be built around five axes:
    - Design / creation / execution
    - Project piloting
    - Production
    - Gifts
    - Production costs
6. Different kinds of street marketing actions include the following:
    - Distributing flyers, a traditional action
    - Product events, re-creating a termporary space to promote a product
    - Human events, where people take over a space and use it to showcase the product
    - Road shows, based on the arrival of new means of transportation
    - Uncovered actions, involving a customization of urban furniture
    - Event actions, temporary mobilization of individuals around dancing, singing or playing
    - Connected objects
7. Street marketing rules:
    - The operation should be sited in a specific location.
    - Strict schedules.
    - Reliance on street marketing professionals.
    - The operation must be visible and transparent.
8. A street marketing campaign must be complemented in the media (using different communications channels) and create a buzz.
9. Street marketing operations' legality must be a permanent focus but attended to on a case-by-case basis.

New Applications of
Street Marketing

Chapter 10

Customizing Street Marketing in Unexpected Ways

Not infrequently, we can find examples online or on social networks of young graduates rebroadcasting street marketing actions in one or several videos, in an attempt to gain companies' favor. Today's job market is so difficult that many people no longer hesitate to use unconventional tools to draw attention to their profiles, capabilities, and know-how.

In a similar vein, personal resumes are often sent nowadays in the form of videos, an idea used by the character Barney in the TV series *How I Met Your Mother*. During one episode, Barney showed his friends a video[1] portraying himself in a very positive light and talking in an offbeat tone. The series' reputation is such that it has been imitated on many occasions, often involving people sharing this particular clip online.

Street marketing responds in many different ways to a wide variety of issues and challenges. In part, this variability reflects changes in the ways that job-offer websites are promoting themselves. The Scholz & Friends communications agency, for instance, once ran a vast campaign in Germany promoting its JobsInTown.de site and showing life-size portraits of robots using customized urban furniture to represent different kinds of workers. The strapline was "Life is too short to do a bad job."[2] The premise had workers replacing machines.

Another example from the field of employment websites involved CareerBuilder, whose promotional campaign targeting desperate job seekers at the end of their tether saw the top of a New York bus decorated with the giant letters "Don't jump."

Streets offer infinite communications possibilities, often conveyed using offbeat and humorous language. Of course, not all communications involve job offers, nor are they all apt to be used by job seekers. At a time when it is increasingly difficult to stand out from other applicants, people need more platforms from whence to see things—and also be seen. As noted by Jacques Froissant, founder of the Altaïde recruitment agency,[3] platforms are constantly evolving, forcing recruiters to find original ways of developing points of contact.

This is the logic behind the English website EmployAdam.com,[4] which people use to upload their resumes and videos. Advertising space promoting the site was rented in the streets of London, generating an immediate buzz with pictures that were retweeted thousands of time. Marketing does not solely consist of selling a product and service but can also cast the spotlight on a person. Given the impact of the economic crisis on employment today, getting a buzz going is almost always the right thing to do. This can be exemplified by two French students who tried to drum up internships by following in the footsteps of Yannick Miel, a young graduate job seeker who had famously offered to "sell himself" on eBay in exchange for a position. Their new idea was to develop a web-based buzz strategy replete with resumes featuring a number of inaccuracies, including a cartoon where the Internet user/recruiter was invited to take off the candidate's clothes to discover his capabilities. The reaction was instantaneous and relayed immediately via social networks, which contributed greatly to the buzz.

For anyone who wants to be innovative and make a splash, marketing has become paramount in how people consume and behave. In today's world, the ability to communicate is the key.

SMEs AND STREET MARKETING

Most small and medium-sized companies face a hard choice. On one hand, to rival larger firms they need to raise their profile using communications campaigns that can be very costly, at a time when the economic crisis requires cost-cutting. On the other hand, many companies understandably consider that it is precisely their strategic communications budget that must be cut. The question for small and medium-sized enterprises (SMEs) therefore becomes how to communicate in a way that will increase their visibility and help them to stand out from the competition without spending a fortune. This explains many SMEs' keen interest in new communications techniques, notably alternative marketing, which allows them to enjoy an innovative and dynamic image while bolstering their attractiveness.

Against this backdrop, it is worth noting the development everywhere of SME operations driven mainly by ingenuity and creativity, with companies emphasizing communications' innovative and fun aspects. We could cite s number of success stories here. One relates to an operation by an American food blender company called Blendtec, whose founder wanted to demonstrate the power of his products and had the idea of filming an iPhone, reputedly very robust, being crushed in his blender. The video spread globally and generated an enormous buzz. The operation was so successful that the man has his own television program today. He also broadcasts online every two weeks a video showing his appliances blending items that are otherwise considered unbreakable. More recently, he tried to blend an iPhone 6 together with a Samsung Galaxy Note 3, using a kind of competitive spirit to show how hard it is mixing things up.

Another American success story involves a simple video featuring Chuck Testa, a taxidermist who wanted to publicize his business.[5] Quickly adopted by crowds of Internet users who are always looking for new uses for videos, Testa created a dedicated YouTube chain full of funny and original parodies. In the end, he got upwards of 14 million views. His success proves that social networks are potentially a powerful market for any kind of company, if only because they reach everywhere. Yet before using them, it is crucial to put together a communications strategy (contents) that can be followed from the beginning to the end of the operation.

Online videoing is not the only technique helping SMEs to succeed, with many highlighting other forms of alternative marketing. A prime example here is Ben & Jerry's, whose founders wagered that they could compete with the giants of the food business not only by selling organic products but also by investing significant sums in alternative marketing, since this would allow them to communicate directly with their core target and with the street. The two upstarts created a tribe loyal to their brand through a number of operations. In 2006, for instance, they walked a cardboard cow through the streets of Paris. In 2008, for 24 hours they had the name of Paris subway station La Motte-Piquet-Grenelle changed to "Michel and Augustin's Banana Plantation," with all curious customers invited to taste their ice cream.

In 2012, Ben and Jerry built another giant cardboard cow bearing their logo in the heart of Paris. Nor did they hesitate to walk around the streets of Paris themselves wearing fabric looking like cowskins. Obviously, all of these operations were pretexts for distributing product samples.

Without a doubt, alternative marketing is well-suited to the different problems inherent to SME communications. Less expensive techniques offer these companies an opportunity to raise their profile and convey an innovative and creative image. Above all, there are many possibilities to choose from. Alternative marketing is much more than simply distributing flyers.

Product promotion events, for example, can be dealt with in a whole variety of ways. In 2008, American company Sto Corp got together in New Orleans with the MLT Creative agency to organize an "improvised" concert featuring a local star, Ben Leathers, playing drums in the street—or to be more specific, playing on yellow pots containing brand products. Rebroadcast on YouTube and generating more than 1,500 views,[6] the operation provides further proof that alternative marketing is perfectly suited to SMEs' communication strategies, and that creativity can be just as effective as, and sometimes even more effective than, using costly media.

Another leading example of a creative operation was that of the German divorce law firm Sabina Stobrawe, which got together with the Gkk Dialoggroup advertising agency in 2008 to promote their expertise by placing stickers representing a bride and groom in their wedding garb on the doors of an elevator, one on the left side and the other on the right. When the doors opened, the spouses separated from one another. In a similar vein, more and more companies are using urban furniture as their support platform. One is DHL, the home delivery firm, which likes to put its famous yellow boxes under urban furniture as if the latter had sprung directly from the former.

Flash mobs, Harlem Shakes and lip dubs (video where actors use playback over existing soundtracks) aimed at promoting a product offer or ideology constitute other techniques that are part of these new alternative communications trends. They have helped a number of SMEs to succeed by raising their profile. Then there is the group of farmers who in 2011 sought to promote their work raising and selling pigs by producing a very funny lip dub at the Rennes Animal Products Fair. This was videoed and re-broadcast online, generating more than 48,000 views on YouTube.[7]

THE EXAMPLE OF DRESR: USING STREET MARKETING TO EXPORT AN AMERICAN START-UP

Newer generations are finding it increasingly difficult to follow what is happening in the fashion industry—consumers find it confusing to have so many different trends. What they are looking for is something simpler, namely how to dress in certain situations. Marketing research shows that many customers look for answers online. The problem is that they are getting such a wide range of responses that it is impossible to know what is best.

One solution is DRESR (www.DRESR.com), a website that gathers all relevant information and creates a place where tastemakers, retailers, and customers can work in harmony creating, sharing, and purchasing fashion. Customers who might otherwise be confused by the plethora of different styles can ask anything they want, as long as it is covered in the website's extensive database. A Pinterest visual discovery model is used to help them in their searches—following which customers can purchase online the outfits they have chosen.

DRESR generally responds to customers' demands by getting trend-setters and retailers to work closely together to advise consumers who might otherwise be lost in the jungle that is the fashion industry. Like any new service or product, DRESR requires new kinds of marketing campaigns, ones based on guerrilla, street, and buzz marketing principles.

The question then becomes how to create street buzz before an online brand is even launched. In a bid to break into the Paris market (one of the world capitals of fashion), the marketing agency with which DRESR was working built a team charged with creating marketing buzz in anticipation of the brand's launch announcement. The consensus view was that street marketing campaigns, a particular focus for the agency in question, are appropriate for generating word-of-mouth. Hence the decision to start a buzz marketing campaign by shooting an operational video. This teaser was meant to reveal the brand's potential video to investors and also critics, whose support was being actively sought. Brainstorming helped the team to define the exact contours of this publicity effort, with a total of five consultants and marketing master's students spending a day in a range of creativity sessions. Around two hundred street marketing operations were conceptualized, with the team using five filters to whittle them down into a shortlist of ten. These filters included creativity; reasonable budget; legality; fit with the overall marketing positioning (fashion, avant-gardism, trendsetters, glitz, technology, etc.) and target; and location. The goal was to end up with a memorable and original event.

Inspired by Christina Aguilera's 2009 perfume campaign and by certain ideas that the team had already suggested for fashion brand Zadig and Voltaire's perfume campaign, the decision was finally made to implement a covered operation customizing urban furniture. DRESR would express itself through customized hangers adorned with invitation cards providing enough information to arouse people's desire and curiosity. The cards would represent the logo (normally a QR code) and slogan: "DRESR, shopping from everywhere." The invitations would be to events taking place at the beginning and end of the September 2014 Paris fashion week. Something similar could subsequently be done in New York and elsewhere—one of the advantages of this approach being its replicability.

Having decided upon the advertising medium, the approach (covered marketing), and the location, the other aims of the operation became clear:

- 300 hangers bearing the sticker "DRESR, shopping from everywhere" were distributed. The code on an invitation card usually facilitates the kind of data monitoring needed to measure the success of an operation. Pre-launch, however, a QR code is useless (because team members cannot measure its impact on sales, etc.).
- A buzz was created around the operation, with a B2B event organized for bloggers and other professionals before the launch.
- A video was shot, to be used both as a teaser and as a fundraising tool.

The dress rehearsal and blank shooting took place in September 2014. A street marketing operation process is always more complicated than a company and its (street) marketing agency thinks. Hence the need to film the proceedings as a control measure. In this case, the street marketing team had to select the right type of hangers, ones befitting the brand's market positioning. It also had to choose the colors best representing the brand and its image (with black and white being the best way of replicating DRESR's logo and website motifs and maintaining its existing traditions). Additionally, ribbons had to be found, lending the event a more sophisticated veneer (with team members opting for a French touch and using French embroidery in reference to DRESR's desire to embrace French culture). Two other points in particular deserve further scrutiny: the requisite legal authorizations; and the storytelling underpinning the video activity.

With respect to the latter, team members sent their storyboard to the video company that had been chosen to record the event and edit the film. After some soul-searching, the company opted for the atmosphere and story that came closest to embodying the company itself: a sunset; Paris' best-known boulevards; fashion styles; zooming techniques; music; and decorations. One excerpt read as follows: "Start with a presentation of the team wearing the most trendsetting outfit possible representing the largest possible group of website users. The scene must be done in slow motion before speeding up to create movement, contours and highlights. The video's third section should show actors' reactions, capturing their surprise, interest and curiosity."

Legal issues were also paramount. It is true that manufacturing shock value without receiving authorization can create a great deal of noise about brand. This strategy has been applied countless times in street marketing, one leading example being the media reaction to an operation where Nike covered the Statue of Liberty in its colors, something that caused a hubbub precisely because the action was illegal. In the case of DRESR, pre-tests were run on Paris' Avenue Montaigne and Avenue Georges V (both situated in the city's affluent luxury goods district) with a view toward selecting the best location. Team members had received police authorization to run the operation (and video it) for two hours. They did it for four.

The blank shooting, done on September 16, helped the marketing team to see a way forward. The agency ended up opting for Avenue Montaigne, because it offers many branded shops (including Louis Vuitton, Chanel, and Dior) and because the fashion week was being run there. Moreover, things played out as expected. The teams ran into difficulties setting up their hanger displays, often being accused of disturbing the ongoing activities of the stores in the area—irrespective of whether authorization had been given or not. On one occasion, a team was told to take its hangers down from a particular store window because the display did not fit in with company policy. In a similar vein, the Canadian embassy asked the teams to leave for security reasons. As for the film crews, they quickly realized that (a) they needed more people filming to capture bystanders' reactions, and (b) the videos were of mediocre quality (if only because tripods were not being used, something that would have ensured less shaky images).

As for bystanders, getting their attention was challenging, if only because most were afraid of interacting with the teams, probably due to a lack of familiarity with ambient marketing. This was somewhat surprising, given that the agency in question had worked on this kind of outdoor marketing operation previously on behalf of famous brands like Thierry Mugler, Swarovsky, David Yurman, Zadig and Voltaire, Porsche design, Azzaro, Clarins, and Diesel. This time around, agency staff had to pretend to be fake bystanders in order to get people involved. This complicated the process, largely because it increased the risk of straying from the storyline that had been worked out beforehand.

DRESR's street marketing operation during the Paris fashion week—and specifically on September 25 and 26, 2014—started with a second shoot being recorded at Rick Owens' Palais de Chaillot show, which started about 6 PM on the first evening. Team members chose this event because, unlike most of the others, it was open to the public, increasing the chances of having a larger audience gaining awareness of the DRESR brand. In addition, the Palais de Chaillot is near the Eiffel Tower and Place du Trocadero, both famous and popular destinations for visitors to Paris.

The team decided to make maximum use of this setting, starting with the large crowds waiting to get into the building before the show began. The obvious solution was to place DRESR hangers on the big gates above the stairs at the front end of Place du Trocadero, since designers, models, journalists, and guests would all be walking through these gates when leaving the show.

Photo 10.1   The DRESR Agency team. (Used by permission, www.streetandmarketing .com; www.lcaconseil.net)

The operation began with potential participants being handed sheets explaining what was happening. The agency also spoke for about ten minutes with Palais de Chaillot Museum's security advisor to explain the purpose of the action. Permission was finally given to display the hangers and record the scene. (Note that requesting authorization for a private event is not the same as for a public space.) Once teams started distributing the hangers, bystanders were instantly attracted to the scene and began taking pictures.

PUBLIC PARTICIPATION

After the operation began, the team suddenly came across a street musician who expressed an interest in DRESR and said he would be happy to wear a few brand DRESR accessories while performing. He also suggested that the agency team talk about the project on his website and upload posts onto his Facebook page. Along with this, as crowd interest in the operation heightened, team members suggested that people take pictures holding the DRESR sign—including models who were passing through the area, something that immediately increased brand visibility. A French TV program called *Le Petit Journal* interviewed one of the team members because she was holding a DRESR invitation card at the very same time that rapper Kanye West was walking past. The

Photo 10.2   The DRESR Hanger operation. (Used by permission, www.streetand marketing.com; www.lcaconseil.net)

interviewer suggested that the agency use the product's location to maximize the brand's exposure. She also recommended that team members be photographed taking pictures by other bloggers or photographers. Lastly, as the hangers were being taken down at the end of the operation, team members starting giving away some of the invitation cards explaining the DRESR concept, directing people to the agency's website so they could see what all the fuss was about.

In short, for however long the operation lasted, agency teams served as DRESR ambassadors. To embody the glamour and respect that the brand represents, they dressed in semi-formal black and white attire, a timeless symbol of class. This also helped team members to be recognized during the operation, making it easier for bystanders to know who to ask questions about the brand. The sum total of these efforts meant that the operation ended up making a big splash.

EVENTS MANAGEMENT AND STREET MARKETING

Events are also communications tools, often ones run outdoors. They consist of organizing a kind of evening or cocktail party, flash mob, etc.—"any sort of happening bringing together anyone involved in the creation, management, promotion or organization of a professional event."[8] A public or private place is chosen, and the event's duration depends on what is involved and the budget. Events can be either cultural or commercial in nature, with the organization being defined by the particular target in question. Many agencies specialize in this kind of communications effort, offering to organize a wide array of events ranging from simple cocktail parties to happenings with more than a hundred persons. Nowadays, their arsenal will also include event actions, which all tend to happen in the open air and often on the street (extreme bicycle racing, paper airplane championships, etc.).

To get the public's attention, brands are increasingly interacting with their audiences, trying to get fans to contribute to events. Brands, organizations, groups, associations, schools, political parties, and companies have all started to do this. The goal is to get people to talk about a company by broadcasting a location where many people have gathered to participate in an event like karaoke, a flash mob, a lip dub, a giant cocktail party, or a giant breakfast—all happenings that can be extremely funny.

One key actor in this arena is Red Bull, a global leader in energy drinks, founded in Austria in 1987 by Dietrich Mateschitz and Chaleo Yoovidhya. Jerôme Lepoivre, who used to work for the brand, has explained that traditional media publicity is not what Red Bull prefers:

"Every year, in the countries where its products are marketed, Red Bull broadcasts at most three television and three radio ads." Yet even if the brand does not have much of a TV ad presence, it is often seen on the television. In France, for instance, viewers can see the brand's logo every Sunday on most channels, given that its owner Dietrich Mateschitz has bought two Formula One racing teams.

The company is, first and foremost, a champion of events marketing. Since its creation, it has sponsored more than three hundred athletes.[9] To avoid becoming prisoner to one type of event and/or to traditional communications, Red Bull has decided to appropriate sporting events— notably, extreme sports. Toward this end, it has spent, according to the Huffington Post,[10] more than 30% of its revenues on events marketing. Red Bull has become a key player in the sports business, positioning itself in specific events such as the Red Bull Air Race, Red Bull Cliff Diving, Red Bull X-Fighters, and Red Bull Crushed Ice[11] while also appealing to wider audiences (sponsoring the New York Red Bull football team)—all events whose costs are minimal compared to traditional advertising campaigns.

CUSTOMIZING THE BUZZ ONLINE

Despite these challenges, companies are in a better position than ever to customize their buzz online. This can largely be explained by the possibility they have of using social networks such as Facebook, Twitter, or YouTube. The customization of buzz marketing has been enabled by the following:

- Generalization of broadband
- Changing ways in which media is used
- Rise of social networks, blogs and online forums

Buzz techniques have gone through a revival ever since everyone started agreeing that they constitute a good online broadcasting strategy. A buzz orientation has the same strengths as guerrilla marketing, if only because it is

- Inexpensive
- Quick to spread
- Customer-oriented
- Deliberate
- Targeted and customized
- Conducive to desire, excitement, curiosity, and a sense of fun

To succeed in customizing a buzz, consumers must be made to feel a rise of adrenaline while forgetting that they are undergoing a marketing operation. This explains why the technique requires so much creativity.

Red Bull recently sponsored one of the craziest events ever in the history of extreme sports: the Red Bull Stratos, when the Austrian parachutist Felix Baumgartner skydived from more than 39 km (24.2 miles) high, at the level of the stratosphere. The cost of this operation is unknown, but its media fallout was phenomenal, with millions of TV viewers watching it worldwide. Twenty-four-hour news stations and radio news programs rebroadcast the event, offering the brand pages of global publicity that it would never have been otherwise able to achieve due to its expense.

To assert the originality of their media complementarity, some companies let fans customize their Facebook pages using brand colors. One case in point is Harley Davidson, which has worked with the Moma Propaganda agency to develop a web browsing application proposing six themes that can be activated and de-activated by simple click. When activated, all the colors on a particular Facebook account can be changed.

Dissemination speed is a key success factor in the customization of buzz. There are many good reasons for doing this online. Economically, it is generally accepted that satisfied customers influence the behavior of two other consumers, whereas dissatisfied ones affect eight other people. The numbers can be enormous across the whole of the Internet, with one satisfied user influencing eight other people. A dissemination speed of this magnitude reveals the power of web media and makes it very understandable why companies might wish to take advantage of this.[12]

Consumers are big players online today. Think back to 2010, when the American clothes giant Gap was experimenting with its new logo. The world's community of Internet users was up in arms, forcing the brand to return to its former logo. Nowadays, these are the people who will be determining whether a particular event succeeds or fails. They will be doing the same with brand notoriety efforts—meaning they will be determining the future impact of most marketing operations.

Chapter 11

Social Causes and the Street

"Ordinary marketers sell in marketplaces. Street marketers sell to people."

Jay Conrad Levinson

Street marketing has turned out to be one of most effective ways of combating traditional marketing's omnipresent advertising. A good street marketing campaign is one that largely convinces the general public by creating an emotional connection between consumers and products.

NGOs AND STREET MARKETING

The main purpose of non-governmental organizations' communications campaigns is to inform the public about the causes they are defending. In parallel, they must also convince people to support their actions. Even if they have different objectives than commercial companies, NGOs face the same problems in devising a successful communications campaign. They too have customers and generate an economic activity. They also need techniques that are as effective as the ones used in mainstream marketing, tools of persuasion that help to convey a coherent message to specific audience. The question that NGOs must therefore answer is to what extent they can continue to satisfy ethical imperatives while using marketing methods.

Street marketing is perfectly adapted to NGOs, since it only requires a small budget. Moreover, using its creative force and nothing else it is

Photo 11.1 Ambient marketing campaign, planned on behalf of the WCPUN (World Council of People at the United Nations). The campaign redirected the use of various statues to focus attention on urban pollution. (Used by permission, www .streetandmarketing.com; www.lcaconseil.net)

Photo 11.2 A WCPUN ambush marketing operation highlighting the need for water protection and mediatizing the New York marathon to communicate a message. (Used by permission, www.streetandmarketing.com; www.lcaconseil.net)

attractive to the public at large (which is more likely to accept this form of communication from an NGO since nothing is being sold). According to Sundar K. Sharma, using the latest communications technologies NGOs can reach a global audience with minimal cost and fewer staff members or less bureaucracy.[1] Indeed, street marketing helps NGOs to meet many of their goals, including:

- Finding the funds needed to develop their activities;
- Mobilizing members, volunteers, and employees;
- Providing information;
- Causing behavioral awareness and change;
- Promoting their actions.

OVERVIEW OF STREET MARKETING FROM AN NGO PERSPECTIVE

Before examining the WWF case study, it is worth looking at four other examples of NGO street marketing:

1. Denver Water Wasting, which pursued a street marketing urban furniture approach in conjunction with a number of groundbreaking conservation programs. The campaign has helped to reduce water consumption by about 20% over the past six years.

2. Eskom used a simple street marketing ad (customizing urban furniture—i.e., a billboard) reminding people to "use electricity wisely"—an interesting message, coming from a utility company.

3. One of UNICEF's global concerns is water accessibility. Toward that end, this major NGO organized a street marketing product event involving the building of a water fountain in the middle of New York City. The water used came from different African countries, with the information boards on the fountain indicating the names of the waterborne diseases that might be caught in each. Nobody drank from the fountain, but many donated to the cause. The action was relayed on television news programs like NY1, as well as in the written press (the *New York Times*, *El Mundo*, CNN's iReport, Omnina.com.mx, porque no. 1, and ADnotas.com). It raised both awareness and funds, engaging more than 7,500 bystanders, attracting global media coverage, and increasing the number of donors beyond all expectations.

4. Action Against Hunger organized a street guerrilla marketing operation involving the transformation of street furniture. The purpose of doing this two days before Paris's March 22 International Water Day was to draw attention to the fact that one-quarter of the world's urban population has no access to drinking water.

THE EXAMPLE OF THE WORLD WILDLIFE FUND (WWF)

The WWF ran an original street marketing campaign in China, trying to make the local population aware of the negative side effects of automobiles' carbon monoxide emissions. A balloon attached to the exhaust pipe of a car driving through the streets of Beijing was shown empty in the morning but filling up over the course of the day. It ended up almost bigger than the car itself, inflated by its emission gases. Once the balloon reached its maximum size, it revealed the message, "The less you drive, the less carbon monoxide in the air you breathe."

In 2005, the WWF conducted another street marketing operation, this time in Brazil, with charity members distributing balloons in the shape of planet Earth, bearing the message, "The world belongs to us." The balloons symbolized fragility in an effort to raise awareness of the importance for future generations of our taking care of planet Earth today.

Among other original campaigns organized by WWF was the "Earth hours" gathering that happened in Switzerland in 2008. On this occasion, the WWF distributed stickers resembling on/off switches in the streets of several cities. The stickers looked so real that many bystanders tried to use them before becoming aware of the WWF message. In parallel, the organization hung posters of pollutant objects or items that use electricity, carrying the message "Do not disturb."

In 2009, the WWF took over a square in the Danish capital Copenhagen and built an ice statue in the form of a life-sized polar bear. The statue melted slowly over the course of the day, revealing the animal's skeleton. Polar bears are threatened more than any other living thing by melting polar ice. The purpose of the operation was to point out global warming's disastrous effects on the world's ecosystems.

Along similar lines, in 2008 WWF undertook an operation where it stuck 1,600 panda-shaped balloons in the ground right in front of the Paris Town Hall. The balloons were inflated using an underground ventilation system. The purpose of the operation was to denounce the negative effects that current lifestyles have on biodiversity, with pandas (an animal at risk of extinction) being the emblem of the WWF.

STREET MARKETING AND POLITICS

Everyone knows about the importance of communications in politics, if only because there have been so many scandals relating to the way in which certain candidates have procured campaign funding. To be seen by as many people as possible, politicians must travel to different cities, organize meetings, and create communications platforms—all of which requires significant investment. Similarly, politicians' supporters and critics also want to be heard. Politicians must convince the widest possible audience that they have good ideas, and they realize that by guaranteeing greater media coverage, quality word-of-mouth (and more generally, alternative marketing) will help them achieve this.

Recent years have seen a resurgence of operations aimed at conveying political messages. Whether they have been organized by a party's supporters or critics, many if not most have adopted alternative marketing campaign codes originating in the world of business. In 2000, for instance, George Bush and John McCain were fighting for the Republican Party's nomination, with each using dog poop as a symbol to show what they thought of the other's program. Bush's opponents went as far as to create flags bearing the slogan "Bush's program" and planting them in piles of dog poop left in public locations across the United States. Aware of this, Bush declared at a press conference toward the end of his second term of office,[2] declaring that his first job after eight years in the White House would be to scoop up dog poop, something that for protocol reasons he had been unable to do until that point.

This increasing use of marketing techniques by the political world is not only happening in the United States. Former French president Nicolas Sarkozy, for instance, undertook an event action during his 2012 electoral campaign, choosing May 1 for his final public meeting before the second round of voting. The event was organized at Paris's Place du Trocadero,[3] with more than 200,000 people scheduled to come and listen. During his speech, Sarkozy talked about the day being for "real workers,"[4] a reference to the fact that his gathering of conservative French supporters from the center-right UMP party (*Union pour un Mouvement Populaire*) took place at the same time as the traditional cortège of labor unions was leaving another part of Paris. Analyzed more deeply, this was an instrumentalization of public spaces and streets that usually host marches but which can also create a sense of togetherness. The event was rebroadcast on giant screens like the ones found at stadium concerts.

Sarkozy and his teams were not the only players to use alternative marketing techniques. Their opponents were also very creative in how they chose to spread their ideas. On March 27, 2010, for instance, a collective flash mob was organized at Paris' Place de la Bastille, with thousands of people creating a human pyramid, called No Sarkozy Day.[5] All wore purple T-shirts, a symbol of political neutrality in France. The action was inspired by the No Berlusconi Day demonstration organized in 2009 in the streets of Rome, when 350,000 people came together to protest against the free market policies of Italy's government at the time.[6]

It is useful to compare this flash mob (a product of alternative marketing) with the aforementioned political meeting. Both had as their main objective the idea of bringing together people who shared an ideology or least common hopes. Both occurred in public spaces and sought to generate word-of-mouth around an operation.

In 2009, at a time when a nepotism scandal was breaking out involving Jean Sarkozy (son of the French president), a flash mob was organized in Paris's La Defense district[7] to denounce the "banana republic" practice of children of powerful parents being parachuted into the highest offices of the land. Participants were invited to wear bananas painted in the colors of the French Republic, pretending they were telephones for ringing the presidential palace in the hope of being appointed to the same high position that Mr. Sarkozy's son had been.

Another example illustrating the similarities between marketing and political actions comes from 2012, when Jean-Luc Melenchon, representing one of France's leading far-left parties, replicated the assault on the Bastille prison that had sparked the French Revolution more than two hundred years previously, organizing a political meeting before the first round of voting.[8] The action brought tens of thousands of people to a location that is highly symbolic for popular demonstrations in France.[9] The Bastille square was overrun by left-wing and far-left activists, sympathizers, and labor unions. The choice of running the operation in the streets, and especially in this particular square, was what gave the event its significance, simultaneously fulfilling the criteria for an event action.

These different examples all illustrate the connections between marketing (and specifically alternative marketing) and politics. Politicians, like companies, must be known and ensure that people remember their names and messages. As in the business world, competition in the political sphere is harsh. Hence the usefulness of mobilizing techniques that have already proved their worth in the field of marketing.

KEY POINTS IN PART 4—NEW APPLICATIONS OF STREET MARKETING

1. Street marketing can help people to find employment.

2. Successful guerrilla street marketing operations can be funny.

3. The customization of online buzz has revived interest in a kind of communications technique that offers a great many advantages (low cost, speed of dissemination, etc.).

4. NGOs and street marketing work well together because both are based on small budgets, creativity, and a desire to interact directly with the public via high-profile campaigns.

5. Political and street marketing happenings are new kinds of public gatherings.

Conclusion: The Outlook for Street Marketing

In general, the concept of street marketing tends to refer to a whole range of mainly promotional approaches that use the street as an experiential platform for consumers interacting with products, brands, professionals, or urban furniture mobilized toward this end. The economic crisis (by encouraging low-cost actions), the explosion of buzz marketing, and the saturation of traditional communications channels are all elements that help to make street marketing a top-quality tool. It is a curious destiny for an old marketing tool that once fell out of favor to now return to the front of the creative scene.

Street marketing primarily consists of putting potential consumer-customers at the heart of all marketing actions, making them the co-creators of what they experience during an operation. This derives directly from marketing's new dominant approach, SDL (Service Dominant Logic[1]), which considers that companies should no longer market *to* consumers but should market *with* them. Companies and consumers' co-creation of value is the key process in this approach. Consumers are transformed into market partners, evolving from spectators to protagonists. This is the crux of recent developments in street marketing, which has gone from being a simple promotional technique to a collaborative marketing tool. It is no longer a question of reaching consumers but of enabling them to play an active part in the event happening in the street.

Street marketing might be perceived as a way of developing experiential approaches linked to brands that no longer wish to stay inside their stores. The thematization of outdoor environments through shows and other temporary (and fun) performances helps companies to nurture experiences that consumers find memorable.[2] In this way, street marketing actions supersede promotions to become a new way of living a brand experience. They create a thematized, hermetic, and secure experiential context in which consumers are happy to immerse themselves.

A brand's street experiences can also become a weapon for brand managers' use, whether in-store, in the factory, at a festival, or online. Consumers have an opportunity to experience the brand's embodiment by connecting directly to it and immersing themselves in it, thereby generating a feeling of proximity and intimacy. Consumers consider these experiences more authentic when they are something that people live rather than a mere commercial transaction. Brands must earn street credibility, a guarantee of authenticity in the eyes of Generation Y consumers. This has become an entire modus operandi for companies like Red Bull, which has undertaken a great many actions in (or relating to) the street.

Red Bull's Street Art View participative operation, created with the help of Google Maps, is a model for this kind of approach.[3] Here everyone can take a picture of street artwork, upload it online, and tag it on site maps by adding GPS data containing the name of the artist and a few bits of information about style. The operation aims to create a memory of street artworks and beautiful graffiti, which often disappear over time as they are covered by other productions. This kind of non-commercial street-based operation gives Red Bull street credibility.

All of this reveals a marketing that does not see itself as marketing—that is, marketing without marketing. In Stephen Brown's reference[4] to the marketing of the new Mini, street marketing is a kind of mini-marketing, based on:

- Mediatization (buzz about non-media actions)
- Inclusion (customers representing companies)
- Nostalgia (references to a time when marketing did not exist)
- Irony (anti-commercial or non-sale approaches)

STREET MARKETING'S EVOLUTION OVER TIME

Alternative marketing has gone into the street. From promotional operations to experiential operations that see sales as the heart of the consumption experience; from product focus in the 1970s to brand focus; from commercial to non-commercial logic based on showmanship; from passive to active consumers (or consummators[5]); from corporate (or American) culture to street culture—these developments have made street marketing into a top-drawer promotional approach in tune with its times. The question is, then, whether this constitutes a new marketing approach or the return of a long-forgotten one.

For thousands of years—long before the word "marketing" was invented—and, indeed, at the beginning of the last century, streets were primarily a locus for business. But they were abandoned in post-war marketing, which preferred supermarkets and malls as places for re-enchanting people with consumption. To re-enchant people with their daily lives today, however, the street must be re-discovered.

And yet, the image of the street has changed. Where once it had a negative connotation, it has transformed nowadays into a place for sociability and contemporary expression, not only for commerce. Indeed, street marketing operations try as hard as possible to obviate the commercial dimension so often associated with streets, drawing from street art inspiration for this. By so doing, they often operate at the borders of illegality, which makes street marketing very attractive to its main target, Generation Y youngsters who tend to resist conventional communications. It is this flirtation with illegality that also makes street marketing so very difficult to implement.

Afterword

I had the pleasure of working with Marcel Saucet on several projects for Clarins Fragrance Group. My first comment is that using street marketing for luxury brands is a somewhat surprising choice. This is a sector where people are accustomed to using traditional marketing techniques (such as celebrities) for communications campaigns.

Before street marketing campaigns began being mediatized to create a buzz—like Kenzo's famous poppy operation—it was unthinkable that luxury brands would seek publicity in the street, if only because streets were not synonymous with luxury. But today our consumers are inundated with advertising messages, and at a time when the economy is struggling, it is vital to stand out from the competition, which can be very harsh at the top of the range. Luxury also needs to surprise its customers—hence its increasing adoption of street marketing, due to this genre's innovative concepts and extreme originality.

Notwithstanding all this, we still face a challenge relating to the means at our disposal to ensure that our communications operations suit our brand's positioning. Where innovation allows us to differentiate, stand out, and create an impactful image meshing with what the market expects of us, relatively unconventional actions like guerrilla or street marketing are still difficult to assess. Having said that (and given Clarins Fragrance Group's attachment to the concept of innovation, whether this involves product R&D or the search for new talent), it seems natural for us to adopt this new vision of marketing—despite the difficulties a large organization such as ourselves may have in assessing its value.

It should be remembered that the new marketing puts consumers at the heart of campaigns. Indeed, this is its strength. Consumers are no longer as passive as they were in the 1980s and 1990s, often viewed as the golden age of communications. Today's campaigns center around consumers and their engagement or involvement. As this book has shown, contemporary brands try to engage audiences through campaign games and activities. But they also try to get people to contribute post-campaign, after the field operation has a ditz run. This is one of the great strengths of innovative marketing. Brands are using participants indirectly as their own relays, implementing buzz strategies relating to the operations that they film, before getting participants to broadcast videos or snapshots through their own social networks—a fabulous shop window for brands. The buzz that can be generated by such events and re-transmitted via social networks and vehicles like YouTube, Vimeo, and DailyMotion is an incredible opportunity for brands to expand their target and reach a much wider audience. Calling on specialist agencies to manage their buzz strategy helps brands to get people to talk about them beyond their customary borders, for a relatively low price. In short, street marketing operations have much greater resonance than any other kind of campaign, offering brands a global shop window without the exorbitant costs of a global campaign based on more traditional communications channels.

This does not mean that the traditional media will be abandoned. It is simply a recognition that street marketing offers brands something that TV, radio, or billboards cannot, namely buzz. Street marketing and buzz are intimately linked today at the dawn of the multi-connected society. They are the future of communications. The attraction here is the splash that marketing makes for a very small investment. This book has shown that many companies have attracted a great deal of spotlight through astonishingly original operations. Taking the decision to launch such operations is commonly associated with luxury brands. As mentioned, Clarins Fragrance Group took time before agreeing to do this. What we also found surprising was the product adaptability that comes with these events. Given the infinite nature of creative persons' imaginations, there has been a perfect adaptation to our creations and the atmospheres that we want to build. Luxury brands, food, cleaning products, airliners, sporting equipment, NGOs, it really does not matter. Thanks to its staging and visual, sound and interactive impact, street marketing can convey all sorts of messages.

It is also important to remember that in today's difficult economic circumstances, this variety of innovative marketing offers a possibility of being constantly present and further investment in communications. Very few brands still have unlimited resources for their communications campaigns. Street marketing obviously requires some financial investment but nothing like the amounts that traditional communications campaigns require.

The main advantage of street marketing lies in creative teams' ability to innovate and nurture brand imagination. Thanks to these professionals, a clever idea can become tomorrow's buzz and touch as many as a million people worldwide. Clearly, it is a great idea to re-situate humans at the heart of marketing campaigns, from design to realization.

Joël Palix, CEO, Feelunique.com

Notes

INTRODUCTION

1. To capture the most representative sample of street marketing operations, we identified both those street marketing campaigns that have had a strong viral impact over the past two years (YouTube, Facebook, Google) as well as their designers, agencies, and/or sponsors. In part, this book is the product of 180 interviews with advertisers (operational marketing directors, product heads, brand managers, sales representatives) and agency managers (directors, project managers, communications managers). The vast majority work out of Paris and its surrounding region.

CHAPTER 1: THE CRISIS IN CONVENTIONAL MARKETING

1. Marcel Saucet, *Innovator: Innover face à la crise* [Innovator: Innovating in the face of crisis] (Nice, France: Editions La tour des Vents, 2009).

2. Jay Conrad Levinson, *Guerrilla Marketing: Easy and Inexpensive Strategies for Making Big Profits from Your Small Business*, Fourth Edition (New York: Houghton Muffin, 2007). See also https://www.youtube.com/watch?v=eQtai7HMbuQ.

3. Levinson, *Guerrilla Marketing*.

4. The marketing mix (or 4 P's) designates, within a product, service, or brand launch framework, a coherent set of decisions relating to the following four policy categories: Product, Price, Place, and Promotion. See E. Jerome McCarthy, *Basic Marketing: A Managerial Approach* (Homewood, IL: Richard D. Irwin, 1960).

5. Didier Gaultier, "Marketing et sortie de crise : un couple plutôt bien assorti!" ["Marketing and crisis management: a well-matched pair!"], JDN (Journal du net), l'economie demain [The economy tomorrow], February 1, 2010, available at http://www.journaldunet.com/ebusiness/expert/44786/mar keting-et-sortie-de-crise---un-couple-plutot-bien-assorti.shtml.

6. "US total media ad spend inches up, pushed by digital," eMarketer .com, August 22, 2013, available at http://www.emarketer.com/Article/US-Total -Media-Ad-Spend-Inches-Up-Pushed-by-Digital/1010154.

7. Ignacio Ramonet, *Propagandes silencieuses* [Silent propaganda] (Paris: Éditions Galilée, 2000).

8. https://www.youtube.com/watch?v=QM9f1buqhLM.

9. Owned by LCAconsulting.net.

CHAPTER 2: UNCONVENTIONAL MARKETING

1. Andreas M. Kaplan and Michael Haenlein, "Two Hearts in Three-Quarter Time: How to Waltz the Social Media Viral Marketing Dance," *Business Horizons* (2001): 54, 3, 253–263.

2. Francesca Casalini and Veronica Vecchi, Impact Iba Investing, SDA Bocconi School of Management (Spring 2011).

3. Philip Kotler is often viewed as the father of modern marketing.

4. Jay Conrad Levinson, *Guerrilla Marketing: Secrets for Making Big Profits from Your Small Business* (New York: Houghton Mifflin, 1984).

5. Kaplan and Haenlein, "Two Hearts."

6. Andrew M. Kaikati and Jack G. Kaikati, "How to Reach Consumers Surreptitiously," *California Management Review* (2001): 46, 4, 6–22.

7. Levinson, *Guerrilla Marketing*.

8. Kaplan and Haenlein, "Two Hearts."

9. Kaplan and Haenlein, "Two Hearts."

10. Rosella C. Gambetti, "Ambient Communication: How to Engage Consumers in Urban Touch-Points," *California Management Review* (2010): 52, 3, 34–51.

11. Abhijit Roy and Satya P. Chattopadhyay, "Stealth Marketing as a Strategy," *Business Horizons* (2010): 53, 1, 69–79.

12. Nicholas Burton and Simon Chadwick, "Ambush Marketing in Sport: An Analysis of Sponsorship Protection Means and Counter-Ambush Measure," *Journal of Sponsorship* (2009): 2, 4, 303–315.

13. Kaplan and Haenlein, "Two Hearts."

14. http://www.youtube.com/watch?feature=player_embedded&v= EQRdE-xlav8.

15. http://www.youtube.com/watch?feature=player_embedded&v= pw00g-m7Dak.

16. Roy and Chattopadhyay, "Stealth Marketing."

17. http://www.ladyplanneuse.com/2010/11/le-stealth-marketing-de-plus -en-plus-la.html.

18. https://www.youtube.com/watch?v=n2Y3GoN2PGw.

19. http://www.youtube.com/watch?feature=player_embedded&v=s_ HUYi9aVvI Site consulté le 19/02/2013.

20. http://www.youtube.com/watch?v=fcaptVbvIIQ.

21. Burton and Chadwick, "Ambush Marketing in Sport."

22. http://yeux-ouverts.blogspot.com/2010/12/le-rugby-fait-son-buzz .html.

23. http://www.ambush-marketing.com/2010/05/abercrombie -ambush-marketing-sur-obama/.

24. "No 'ambush marketing': mouthguard maker," *New Zealand Herald,* October 5, 2011, available at http://www.nzherald.co.nz/business/news/article .cfm?c_id=3&objectid=10756641.

25. http://www.youtube.com/watch?v=Bnn2h6tEhjA&feature=pla yer_embedded.

26. Gambetti, "Ambient Communication."

27. http://jedblogk.blogspot.com/2009/08/hubba-bubba.html.

28. http://www.paperblog.fr/1096570/une-armee-de-chucky -affole-new-york/.

29. http://www.from-paris.com/touchez-du-bois-ca-peut-vous-porter -chance-loto/.

30. Kaplan and Haenlein, "Two Hearts."

31. Gambetti, "Ambient Communication."

32. Sophie Rieunier, *Le Marketing sensoriel du point de vente* [Sensory marketing at the point of sale] (Paris: Dunod, 2006).

33. Gambetti, "Ambient Communication."

34. Ibid.

35. http://likeshareadd.wordpress.com/2011/02/12/floorgraphic-get -them-off-your-dog/.

36 Levinson, *Guerrilla Marketing.*

37 Yohan Gicquel, *Le street marketing* [Street marketing] (Paris: Éditions Le génie des glaciers, 2006).

38. Jean-Marc Lehu, *L'Encyclopédie du marketing* [The encyclopedia of marketing] (Paris: Éditions d'Organisation, 2004).

39. Gambetti, "Ambient Communication."

40. Lehu, *L'Encyclopédie du marketing.*

41. Jan Brace-Govan and Helene De Burgh-Woodman, "Sneakers and Street Culture: A Postcolonial Analysis of Marginalized Cultural Consumption," *Consumption Markets & Culture* (2008): 11, 2, 93–112.

42. "Subversive activity that changes the use of a public space and invents relatively paradoxical forms of expression that might be called capitalist surrealism or postmodern realism, and which change how communications are done," according to Luca M. Visconti, John F. Sherry Jr., Stefania Borghini, and Laurel Anderson, "Street Art, Sweet Art: The Reclamation of Public Place," *Journal of Consumer Research* (2010): 37, 3, 511–529.

43. Stefania Borghini, Luca M. Visconti, Laurel Anderson, and John F. Sherry Jr., "Symbiotic Postures of Commercial Advertising and Street Art: Implications for Creativity," *Journal of Advertising* (2010): 39, 3, 115–128.

44.   Olivier Cathus (1998), *L'âme-sueur. Le funk and les musiques populaires du XXᵉ siècle* [Soul-sweat: Funk and the popular music of the twentieth century] (Paris: Éditions Desclée de Brouwer, 1998).

45.   Visconti, Sherry, Borghini, and Anderson, "Street Art, Sweet Art."

CHAPTER 3: REIMAGINING THE STREET

1.   http://www.mansgreatestmistake.com/the-politics-of-cars/reclaim-the-streets (August 27, 2012).

2.   Catherine Aventin, "Les arts de la rue pour observer, comprendre and aménager l'espace public" ["The art of the street, to observe, understand and develop public space"], *TIGR* (*Travaux de l'Institut de géographie de Reims* [Works of the Geography Institute of Reims]), nos. 119–120, "Nouvelles approches de l'espace dans les sciences de l'homme and de la société" [New approaches to space in the human and social sciences], University of Reims Champagne-Ardenne, (2006): 9, 4.

3.   Diana Derval, *Wait Marketing: communiquer au bon moment, au bon endroit* [Wait Marketing: Communicating at the right moment, in the right place] (Paris: Éditions Eyrolles, 2006).

4.   Diet Coke Presents: The Slender Vender (sic), https://www.youtube.com/watch?v=wyYuXxccTWU.

5.   Eric Blin, "Les repas de la rue: émergence d'une nouvelle fête urbaine ou effet de mode? L'example de Tours" [Street meals: emergence of a new urban celebration or effect of fashion?], in *Norois*, 207, (2008):2, 85–96, 94.

6.   Stefania Borghini, Luca M. Visconti, Laurel Anderson, and John F. Sherry Jr., "Symbiotic Postures of Commercial Advertising and Street Art: Implications for Creativity," *Journal of Advertising* (2010): 39, 3, 115–128.

7.   D'Emannuelle Lallement, *La ville marchande: enquête à Barbès* [The market town: survey of Barbès] (Paris: Téraèdre, 2010).

8.   Jan Brace-Govan and Helene De Burgh-Woodman, "Sneakers and Street Culture: A Postcolonial Analysis of Marginalized Cultural Consumption," *Consumption Markets & Culture* (2008): 11, 2, 93–112.

9.   Luca M. Visconti, John F. Sherry Jr., Stefania Borghini, and Laurel Anderson "Street Art, Sweet Art: The Reclamation of Public Place," *Journal of Consumer Research* (2010): 37, 3, 511–529.

10.   Olivier Cathus, *L'âme-sueur. Le funk and les musiques populaires du XXᵉ siècle* [Soul-sweat: Funk and the popular music of the twentieth century] (Paris: Éditions Desclée de Brouwer, 1998).

11.   Michael Maffesoli, *The Time of the Tribes* (London: Sage, 1996); Bernard Cova, "Community and Consumption: Towards a Definition of the Linking Value of Products or Services," *European Journal of Marketing* (1997): 31, 3/4, 297–316.

12.   John F. Sherry Jr., Robert V. Kozinets, and Stefania Borghini, "Agents in Paradise: Experiential Co-Creation through Emplacement, Ritualization, and Community," in Antonella Carù and Bernard Cova, eds., *Consuming Experiences* (London: Routledge, 2007), 17–33.

13. Pierre R. Berthon, Leyland F. Pitt, Ian McCarthy, and Steven M. Kates, "When Customers Get Clever: Managerial Approaches to Dealing with Creative Consumers," *Business Horizons* (2007) 50, 39–47.

14. Ibid.

15. George Ritzer, Paul Dean, and Nathan Jurgenson, "The Coming Age of the Prosumer," *American Behavioral Scientist* (April 2012) 56: 379–398.

16. Stephen L. Vargo and Robert F. Lusch, "Evolving to a New Dominant Logic for Marketing," *Journal of Marketing* (2004) 68:1, 1–18.

17. George Ritzer and Nathan Jurgenson, "Production, Consumption, Prosumption: The Nature of Capitalism in the Age of the Digital 'Prosumer,'" *Journal of Consumer Culture* (2010): 10, 1, 13–36.

18. Martin Kornberger, *Brand Society: How Brands Transform Management and Lifestyle* (Cambridge, U.K.: Cambridge University Press, 2010).

19. Mark D. Uncles, "Know Thy Changing Consumer," *Journal of Brand Management* (2008): 15, 4, 227–231.

20. Alex Wipperfürth, *Brand Hijack: Marketing without Marketing* (New York: Portfolio, 2005).

21. Berthon, Pitt, McCarthy, and Kates, "When Customers Get Clever," 47.

22. Thomas C. O'Guinn and Albert M. Muñiz, Jr., "Communal Consumption and the Brand," in *Inside Consumption: Frontiers of Research on Consumer Motives, Goals, and Desires*, David Glen Mick and S. Ratneshwar (eds.) (New York: Routledge, 2005), 252–272.

23. Robert V. Kozinets, Andrea Hemetsberger, Hope J. Schau, "The Wisdom of Consumer Crowds: Collective Innovation in the Age of Networked Marketing," *Journal of Macromarketing* (2008): 28, 4, 339–354.

24. Bernard Cova and Daniele Dalli, "Working Consumers: The Next Step in Marketing Theory?" *Marketing Theory* (2009): 9, 3, 315–339.

25. Eric von Hippel, "Lead Users: A Source of Novel Product Concepts," *Management Science* (1986): 32, 791–805; Eric von Hippel, *Democratizing Innovation* (Cambridge, MA: MIT Press, 2005).

26. Nikolaus Franke, Eric von Hippel, and Martin Schreier, "Finding Commercially Attractive User Innovations: A Test of Lead-User Theory," *Journal of Product Innovation Management* (2006): 23, 4, 301–315.

27. Johann Fuller, Gregor Jawecki, and Hans Muhlbacher, "Innovation Creation by Online Basketball Communities," *Journal of Business Research* (2007): 60, 1, 60–71; see also Gianluca Marchi, Claudio Giachetti, Pamela De Gennaro, "Extending Lead-User Theory to Online Brand Communities: The Case of the Community Ducati," *Technovision* (2011): 31, 8, 350–361; Emanuela Prandelli, Gianmario Verona, and Deborah Raccagni, "Diffusion of Web-Based Product Innovation," *California Management Review* (2006): 48, 4, 109–135; Mohanbir Sawhney, Gianmario Verona, and Emanuela Prandelli, "Collaborating to Create: The Internet as a Platform for Customer Engagement in Product Innovation," *Journal of Interactive Marketing,* (2005): 19, 4, 4–17.

28. Sawhney, Verona, and Prandelli, "Collaborating to Create"; Marchi, Giachetti, and De Gennaro, "Extending Lead-User Theory."

29. O'Guinn and Muñiz, "Communal Consumption and the Brand."

30. Vargo and Lusch, "Evolving to a New Dominant Logic for Marketing."

31. Coimbatore K. Prahalad and Venkatram Ramaswamy, "Co-creating Unique Value with Customers," *Strategy & Leadership* (2004): 32, 3, 4–9.

32. Adam Arvidsson, *Brands: Meaning and Value in Media Culture* (London: Routledge, 2006).

33. Pierre Berthon, Leyland F. Pitt, and Colin Campbell, "Ad Lib: When Customers Create the Ad," *California Management Review* (2008): 50, 4, 6–30.

34. Mary J. Hatch and Majken Schultz, "Toward a Theory of Brand Co-Creation with Implications for Brand Governance," *Journal of Brand Management* (2010): 17, July/August, 590–604.

35. http://trendwatching.com/trends/CUSTOMER-MADE.htm.

CHAPTER 4: WHERE THE STREET GENERATES A MODERN CULTURE

1. M. Berger and V. Morlet, "Le flash mob en hommage á Mandela dans un supermarché de Pretoria" [The flash mob in honor of Mandela in a supermarket in Pretoria] (December 12, 2013), http://www.rtbf.be/info/medias/dossier/vu-sur-le-web/detail_le-flash-mob-en-hommage-a-mandela-dans-un-supermarche-de-pretoria?id=8156119.

2. http://youtu.be/9OawiTae0bA.

3. Jerry Welsh invented the term in the 1980s while working for American Express. Today he is a seminal reference in the field of events communications and is considered an expert in the use of sponsoring in marketing.

4. David Shani and Dennis M. Sandler, "Ambush Marketing: Is Confusion to Blame for the Flickering or the Flame?" *Psychology & Marketing* (1998) 15: 367–383.

CHAPTER 5: THE STREET AND WORD-OF-MOUTH

1. Walter J. Carl, "What's All the Buzz About? Everyday Communication and the Relational Basis of Word-of-Mouth and Buzz Marketing Practices," *Management Communication Quarterly* (2006), 19, 4, 601–634.

2. Justin Kirby and Paul Marsden, *Connected Marketing: The Viral, Buzz and Word-of-Mouth Revolution* (Jordan Hill, Oxford: Elsevier Linacre House, 2006), 275.

3. https://www.pinterest.com/pin/517632550893857870/.

4. Below-the-line actions are non-media-related—unlike above-the-line operations, which use the mainstream media and whose outcomes can be monitored.

CHAPTER 6: AN EVOLVING PRACTICE

1. Jay C. Levinson (1984), op cit.

2. Jean-Marc Lehu, *L'Encyclopédie du marketing* [The encyclopedia of marketing] (Éditions d'Organisation, 2004, 2012).

3. https://www.pinterest.com/pin/484911084850486675/.
4. http://fr.lush.eu/shop/info/11/lush-nous-croyons.
5. http://www.blog-note.com/publicite-de-fedex-contre-ups/.
6. http://www.youtube.com/watch?v=segMdfc3U3s.
7. http://www.zapiks.fr/red-bull-contest-2008.html.

CHAPTER 7: CREATING A STREET MARKETING CAMPAIGN

1. A "Be Womanity" bus (operation carried out by Be and Thierry Mugler) ran into a hiccup when it started snowing. Bystanders had to wait a long time in the snow before they could get on the bus.

2. The study preceded the operations but also continued afterward, in order to get participant feedback about its suitability, including people's vision of the brand and its products.

3. Undercover actions are, by their very nature, discreet and based on subliminal brand marketing. It is important that they do not resemble a promotional action but focus on piquing consumers' curiosity.

CHAPTER 8: GENERATING BUZZ

1. http://youtu.be/Txn_8V1yZ2Y.
2. http://www.marketing-alternatif.com/2007/05/22/nissan-350z-trains-new-engine/.
3. http://www.crankycreative.com/sandbox/blog/bid/20258/Snake-Bus-Wrap-Copenhagen-Zoo.
4. http://www.ibelieveinadv.com/commons/ParissaBackvertising.jpg.
5. http://scaryideas.com/content/9828/.
6. http://www.motivators.com/images/blogimages/alot-more-than-promos/windex.jpg.
7. http://www.marketing-alternatif.com/2007/02/22/amnesty-international-espagne/.
8. http://www.lepoint.fr/societe/une-action-au-louvre-pour-ne-pas-rester-de-glace-face-au-sort-des-sdf-08-07-2010-1212645_23.php.
9. http://www.w3sh.com/2009/01/21/dont-step-into-danger/.
10. http://artofstreetmarketing.wordpress.com/tag/k2r/.
11. http://www.tout-paris.org/des-canapes-ikea-dans-le-metro-8057.
12. See the images of this operation at the beginning of this book. http://youtu.be/thu9zpzrZz0.
13. http://youtu.be/rULU0luQIVU.
14. https://www.youtube.com/watch?v=R-L4QKMUvpo.
15. http://www.youtube.com/watch?v=71E3xE0a4ZI.
16. Andreas M. Kaplan and Michael Haenlein, "Two Hearts in Three-Quarter Time: How to Waltz The Social Media Viral Marketing Dance," *Business Horizons* (2001) 54: 3, 253–263.
17. Iain Black and Iain Nevill, "Fly-posting: An Investigation of a 'Controversial' Medium," *Journal of Marketing Communication* (2009) 15, 4, 209–226.

CHAPTER 9: EVALUATING RISK

1. Iain Black and Iain Nevill, "Fly-posting: An Investigation of a 'Controversial' Medium," *Journal of Marketing Communication* (2009) 15, 4: 209–26.

2. Luca M. Visconti, John F. Sherry Jr., Stefania Borghini, and Laurel Anderson, "Symbiotic Postures of Commercial Advertising and Street Art: Implications for Creativity," *Journal of Advertising* (2010) 39, 3, 115–128. See also Jan Brace-Govan and Helene De Burgh-Woodman, "Sneakers and Street Culture: A Postcolonial Analysis of Marginalized Cultural Consumption," *Consumption Markets & Culture*, 11, 2, 93–112.

3. Brace-Govan and De Burgh-Woodman, "Sneakers and Street Culture."

4. Douglas West and John Ford, "Advertising Agency Philosophies and Employee Risk Taking," *Journal of Advertising* (2001) 30, 1: 77–91.

5. Jaber F. Gubrium and James A. Holstein, *Postmodern Interviewing* (Thousand Oaks, CA: Sage, 2003).

6. Shadd Maruna and Heith Copes, "What have we learned from five decades of neutralization research?" *Crime and Justice* (2005) 32: 221–320.

7. Maria G. Piacentini, Andreas Chatzidakis, and Emma N. Banister, "Making Sense of Drinking: The Role of Techniques of Neutralization and Counter-Neutralization in Negotiating Alcohol Consumption," *Sociology of Health and Illness* (2012) 34, 6.

8. Ruwen Ogien, *L'éthique Aujourd'hui: Maximalistes and Minimalistes* [Ethics today: Maximalists and minimalists] (Paris: Gallimard, 2007).

9. Ibid.

10. Rodolphe Durand and Jean-Philippe Vergne, *The Pirate Organization: Lessons from the Fringes of Capitalism* (Boston: Harvard Business Review Press, 2012).

11. Kelly D. Martin and Craig Smith, "Commercializing Social Interaction: The Ethics of Stealth Marketing," *Journal of Public Policy & Marketing*, (2008) 27, 1: 45–56.

12. Martin and Smith, "Commercializing Social Interaction." See also Ross D. Petty and Craig Andrews, "Covert Marketing Unmasked: A Legal and Regulatory Guide for Practices That Mask Marketing Messages," *Journal of Public Policy & Marketing* (2008) 27, 1: 7–18.

13. Luc Boltanski and Laurent Thévenot [1991 French Edition], *On Justification: Economies of Worth* (Princeton: Princeton University Press, 2006).

14. Jay C. Levinson, Frank Adkins, and Chris Forbes, *Guerrilla Marketing for Non-Profits* (Irvine, CA: Entrepreneurs Media, 2010).

15. Martin and Smith, "Commercializing Social Interaction."

16. Michael Beverland, Francis Farrelly, and Zeb Woodhatch, "Exploring the Dimensions of Proactivity within Advertising Agency–Connection Relationship," *Journal of Advertising* (2007) 36, 4: 49–60.

17. West and Ford, "Advertising Agency Philosophies."

18. Stefania Borghese, Luca M. Visconti, Laurel Anderson, and John F. Sherry Jr., "Street Art, Sweet Art: The Reclamation of Public Place," *Journal of Consumer Research* (2010) 37, 3, 511–529.

19. Black and Nevill, "Fly-posting."

20. Piacentini, Chatzidakis, and Banister, "Making Sense of Drinking."

21. Bernard Cova, "Le généricide des marques: leurre ou menace réelle?" [The genericide of brands: Lure or real threat?] *Décisions Marketing* (2013) 71:111–123.

22. *Metromedia, Inc. v. City of San Diego*, 453 U.S. 490, 101 S. Ct. 2882, 69 L. Ed. 2d 800 (1981), see Plaintiff's Statement of the Case, 2: 10 – 16, June 25, 2013.

23. Ibid.

24. Ibid.

25. Ibid.

26. Ibid.

27. Ibid.

28. The popular (and anonymous) street artist Banksy coined the term "brandalism" in his film *Exit Through the Gift Shop* by stating: "Any advertisement in public space that gives you no choice as to whether you see it or not ... belongs to you. It's yours to take, rearrange, and reuse. Asking for permission is like asking to keep a rock that someone just threw at your head."

29. Cal. Penal Code §594(a)(b)(2)(A).

30. http://www.huffingtonpost.com/2013/07/02/jeff-olson-san-diego -chalk-_n_3532834.html; http://rt.com/usa/vandalism-san-olson-diego-506/.

31. Bernard Cova and Marcel Saucet, "Unconventional Marketing: From Guerrilla to Consumer Made," in *Routledge Companion on The Future of Marketing* (London: Routledge, 2013).

32. Ibid.

33. Maruna and Copes, "What Have We Learned?"

34. Piacentini, Chatzidakis, and Banister, "Making Sense of Drinking."

35. Ogien, *L'éthique Aujourd'hui.*

36. Ibid.

37. Durand and Vergne, *The Pirate Organization.*

38. Martin and Smith, "Commercializing Social Interaction."

39. Cova and Saucet, "Unconventional Marketing."

40. Boltanski and Thévenot, *On Justification.*

41. Winston Tellis, "Application of a Case Study Methodology," *The Qualitative Report* (September 1997), 3, 3.

42. http://www.rentabiliweb.com/fr/.

CHAPTER 10: CUSTOMIZING STREET MARKETING IN UNEXPECTED WAYS

1. https://www.youtube.com/watch?v=GuLcxg5VGuo.

2. http://nonidesign.over-blog.com/article-street-marketing-pour-l -emploi-65973473.html.

3. http://www.lexpress.fr/emploi-carriere/emploi/pour-trouver-un -emploi-faites-tout-pour-rencontrer-les-recruteurs_1108655.html See also the French edition of the book, by Jay Conrad Levinson and David E.Perry, adapted by Jacques Froissant, Guerrilla Marketing pour trouver un emploi [Guerilla marketing to find a job] (Paris: Éditions Diateino, 2012).

4. http://www.cv-originaux.fr/2013/01/03/louer-panneau-publicitaire
-faire-un-cv-video-et-creer-un-site-dedie-adam-pacitti-veut-un-job/.

5. http://www.youtube.com/user/ojaivalleytaxidermy.

6. http://www.youtube.com/watch?v=F7mXhFslxjw.

7. http://www.youtube.com/watch?v=TdJOZV3UA1k.

8. http://www.heavent-expo.com/A+propos_756.html.

9. http://www.lexpress.fr/actualite/societe/l-eacute-nergique-mr-red
-bull_481267.html.

10. http://www.huffingtonpost.fr/2012/10/15/red-bull-stratos-felix
-baumgartner-khris_n_1966124.html.

11. http://www.redbull.fr/cs/Satellite/fr_FR/World-Series/00124274
6062432.

12. Pricille Opsome and Gwennaëlle Bizien, *Les nouvelles tendances du
marketing : le buzz marketing* [New trends in marketing: buzz marketing]
(YouScribe, 2012).

CHAPTER 11: SOCIAL CAUSES AND THE STREET

1. Sundar K. Sharma, "Reviewing NGOs' Media Strategies: Possibilities
for NGO–Media Collaboration," *Human and Natural Resources Studies*
(Kathmandu University, Nepal, 2010).

2. http://lci.tf1.fr/insolite/2010-10/georges-bush-de-la-maison-blanche
-aux-crottes-de-chien-6109416.html.

3. http://tempsreel.nouvelobs.com/election-presidentielle-2012/20120501
.OBS7445/au-trocadero-nicolas-sarkozy-revendique-un-1er-mai-tricolore.html.

4. http://elections.lefigaro.fr/flash-presidentielle/2012/04/23/97006
-20120423FILWWW00483-sarkozy-organise-un-rassemblement-le-1er-mai.php.

5. http://www.leparisien.fr/politique/faible-mobilisation-pour-le-no-sar
kozy-day-27-03-2010-865786.php.

6. http://www.lemonde.fr/europe/portfolio/2009/12/05/succes-en-italie
-pour-le-no-berlusconi-day_1276707_3214.html.

7. http://tempsreel.nouvelobs.com/politique/20091022.OBS5483/un
-flash-mob-moque-jean-sarkozy-a-la-defense.html.

8. http://www.bfmtv.com/politique/place-comble-a-la-bastille-ou-melen
chon-a-tenu-un-grand-meeting-208813.html.

9. http://www.lexpress.fr/actualite/politique/a-la-bastille-melenchon
-reussit-son-pari_1095014.html.

CONCLUSION: THE OUTLOOK FOR STREET MARKETING

1. Stephen L. Vargo and Robert F. Lusch, "Evolving to a New Dominant
Logic for Marketing," *Journal of Marketing* (2004) 68, 1, 1–18.

2. John F. Sherry Jr., Robert V. Kozinets, and Stefania Borghini, "Agents
in Paradise: Experiential Co-Creation through Emplacement, Ritualization, and
Community," in Antonella Carù and Bernard Cova, eds., *Consuming Experiences*
(London: Routledge, 2007) 17–33.

3.   www.streetartview.com.

4.   Stephen Brown, "O Customer, Where Art Thou?" *Business Horizons* (2004) 47, 4, 61–67.

5.   Marcel Saucet and Savario Tomasella, "La marque consommée" [The brand consumed], Fifth Normandy conference on Consumption and Societies Research, IAE de Caen, March 23-24, 2006; Marcel Saucet, "Le diamant: une veille stratégique sensorielle." Strategic, Scientific and Technological Watch conference, Université Toulouse 3, October 26, 2004.

Bibliography

Arvidsson, Adam (2006), *Brands: Meaning and Value in Media Culture.* London: Routledge.

Aventin, Catherine (2006), "Les arts de la rue pour observer, comprendre et aménager l'espace public" [The art of the street to observe, understand, and manage public space] TIGR (Travaux de l'Institut de géographie de Reims [Works of the Geographical Institute of Reims]), 119–120, dossier "Nouvelles approches de l'espace dans les sciences de l'homme et de la société" [New approaches to space in the human and social sciences], Université de Reims Champagne-Ardenne, 9, p. 4.

Berthon, Pierre, Leyland Pitt, and Colin Campbell (2008), "Ad Lib: When Customers Create the Ad," *California Management Review,* 50, 4, 6–30.

Berthon, Pierre, Leyland Pitt, Ian McCarthy, and Steven M. Kates (2007), "When Customers Get Clever: Managerial Approaches to Dealing with Creative Consumers," *Business Horizons* 50, 39–47.

Beverland, Michael, Francis Farrelly, and Zeb Woodhatch (2007), "Exploring the Dimensions of Proactivity within Advertising Agency–Client Relationships," *Journal of Advertising,* 36, 4, 49–60.

Black, Iain, and Iain Nevill (2009), "Fly-posting: An Investigation of a 'Controversial' Medium," *Journal of Marketing Communication* 15, 4, 209–226.

Blin, Eric (2008), "Les repas de rue : émergence d'une nouvelle fête urbaine ou effet de mode? L'exemple de Tours" [The street meal: emergence of a new urban feast or effect of fashion?], *Norois,* 207, 2008/2, 85–96.

Boltanski, Luc, and Laurent Thévenot (2006) [1991 French Edition], *On Justification: Economies of Worth,* Princeton: Princeton University Press.

Borghini, Stefania, Luca M. Visconti, Laurel Anderson, and John F. Sherry Jr. (2010), "Symbiotic Postures of Commercial Advertising and Street Art: Implications for Creativity," *Journal of Advertising,* 39, 3, 115–128.

Brace-Govan, Jan, and Helene De Burgh-Woodman (2008), "Sneakers and Street Culture: A Postcolonial Analysis of Marginalized Cultural Consumption," in *Consumption Markets & Culture*, 11, 2, 93–112.

Brown, Stephen (2004), "O Customer, Where Art Thou?" *Business Horizons*, 47, 4, 61–70.

Burton, Nicholas, and Simon Chadwick (2009), "Ambush Marketing in Sport: An Analysis of Sponsorship Protection Means and Counter-Ambush Measures," in *Journal of Sponsorship*, 2, 4, 303–315.

Carl, Walter J. (2006), "What's All the Buzz About? Everyday Communication and the Relational Basis of Word-of-Mouth and Buzz Marketing Practices," *Management Communication Quarterly*, 19, 4, 601–634.

Cathus, Olivier (1998), *L'âme-sueur: Le funk et les musiques populaires du XXe siècle* [Soul-sweat: funk and the popular music of the twentieth century], Paris: Éditions Desclée de Brouwer.

Cova, Bernard (1997), "Community and Consumption: Towards a Definition of the Linking Value of Products or Services," *European Journal of Marketing*, 31, 3/4, 297–316.

Cova, Bernard, and Daniele Dalli (2009), "Working Consumers: The Next Step in Marketing Theory?" *Marketing Theory* 9, 3, 315–339.

Cova, Bernard, and Marcel Saucet (2013), "The Secret Lives of Unconventional Campaigns: Street Marketing on the Fringe," *Journal of Marketing Communications: Special Issue on Ambient/Street Marketing*.

Derval, Diana (2006), *Wait Marketing: communiquer au bon moment, au bon endroit* [Wait marketing: communicating at the right moment, in the right place], Paris: Éditions Eyrolles.

Durand, Rodolphe, and Jean-Philippe Vergne (2012), *The Pirate Organization: Lessons from the Fringes of Capitalism*, Boston: Harvard Business Press.

Franke, Nikolaus, Eric von Hippel, and Martin Schreier (2006), "Finding Commercially Attractive User Innovations: A Test of Lead-User Theory," *Journal of Product Innovation Management*, 23, 4, 301–315.

Fuller, Johann, Gregor Jawecki, and Hans Muhlbacher (2007), "Innovation Creation by Online Basketball Communities," *Journal of Business Research*, 60, 1, 60–71.

Gambetti, Rosella C. (2010), "Ambient Communication: How to Engage Consumers in Urban Touch-Points," *California Management Review* 52, 3, 34–51.

Gicquel, Yohan (2006), *Le street marketing* [Street marketing], Paris: Éditions Le génie des glaciers.

Gubrium, Jaber F., and James A. Holstein (2003), *Postmodern Interviewing*, Thousand Oaks, CA: Sage.

Hasley, Mark, and Alison Young (2006), "Our Desires Are Ungovernable: Writing Graffiti in Urban Space," *Theoretical Criminology* 10, 3, 275–306.

Hatch, Mary J., and Majken Schultz (2010), "Toward a Theory of Brand Co-Creation with Implications for Brand Governance," *Journal of Brand Management*, 17, July/August, 590–604.

Kaikati, Andrew M., and Jack G. Kaikati (2004), "How to Reach Consumers Surreptitiously," *California Management Review*, 46, 4, 6–22.

Kaplan, Andreas M., and Michael Haenlein (2001), "Two Hearts in Three-Quarter Time: How to Waltz the Social Media Viral Marketing Dance," *Business Horizons*, 54, 3, 253–263.

Kirby, Justin, and Paul Marsden (2006), *Connected Marketing: The Viral, Buzz, and Word-of-Mouth Revolution*, Elsevier Linacre House, Jordan Hill, Oxford.

Kornberger, Martin (2010), *Brand Society: How Brands Transform Management and Lifestyle*, Cambridge, U.K.: Cambridge University Press.

Kozinets, Robert V., Andrea Hemetsberger, and Hope J. Schau (2008), "The Wisdom of Consumer Crowds: Collective Innovation in the Age of Networked Marketing," *Journal of Macromarketing*, 28, 4, 339–354.

Kutsch, Elmar (2010), "Deliberate Ignorance in Project Risk Management," *International Journal of Project Management*, 28, 3, 245–255.

Lallement, D'Emmanuelle (2010), *La ville marchande: enquête à Barbès* [The market town: survey of Barbès]. Paris: Téraèdre.

Lehu, Jean-Marc (2004), *L'Encyclopédie du marketing* [The encyclopedia of marketing], Paris: Éditions d'Organisation.

Levinson, Jay C. (1984), *Guerrilla Marketing, Secrets for Making Big Profits from your Small Business*, New York: Houghton Mifflin.

Levinson, Jay C., Frank Adkins, and Chris Forbes (2010), *Guerrilla Marketing for Non Profit*. Irvine, CA: Entrepreneurs Media.

Maffesoli, Michel (1996), *The Time of the Tribes*, Sage: London.

Marchi, Gianluca, Claudio Giachetti, Pamela De Gennaro (2011), "Extending Lead-User Theory to Online Brand Communities: The Case of the Community Ducati," *Technovision*, 31, 8, 350–361.

Martin, Kelly D., and Craig Smith (2008), "Commercializing Social Interaction: The Ethics of Stealth Marketing," *Journal of Public Policy & Marketing*, 27, 1, 45–56.

Maruna, Shadd, and Heith Copes (2005), "What Have We Learned from Five Decades of Neutralization Research?" *Crime and Justice*, 32, 221–320.

Ogien, Ruwen (2007), *L'éthique Aujourd'hui: Maximalistes et Minimalistes* [Ethics today: maximalists and minimalists]. Paris: Gallimard.

O'Guinn, Thomas C., and Albert M. Muñiz Jr. (2005), "Communal Consumption and the Brand," *Inside Consumption: Frontiers of Research on Consumer Motives, Goals, and Desires*, David Glen Mick and S. Ratneshwar (eds.), New York: Routledge, 252–272.

Opsome, Pricille, and Gwennaëlle Bizien (2012), *Les nouvelles tendances du marketing: le buzz marketing* [New trends in marketing: buzz marketing], YouScribe.

Petty, Ross D., and Craig J. Andrews (2008), "Covert Marketing Unmasked: A Legal and Regulatory Guide for Practices that Mask Marketing Messages," *Journal of Public Policy & Marketing* 27, 1, 7–18.

Piacentini, Maria G., Andreas Chatzidakis, and Emma N. Banister (2012), "Making Sense of Drinking: The Role of Techniques of Neutralisation and Counter-Neutralisation in Negotiating Alcohol Consumption," in *Sociology of Health and Illness*, 34, 6.

Prahalad, Coimbatore K., and Venkatram Ramaswamy (2004), "Co-creating Unique Value with Customers," *Strategy & Leadership*, 32, 3, 4–9.

Prandelli, Emanuela, Gianmario Verona, and Deborah Raccagni (2006), "Diffusion of Web-Based Product Innovation," *California Management Review*, 48, 4, 109–135.

Ramonet, Ignacio (2000), *Propagandes silencieuses* [Silent propaganda], Paris: Éditions Galilée.

Rieunier, Sophie (2006), *Le Marketing sensoriel du point de vente* [Sensory marketing at the point of sale], Paris: Éditions Dunod.

Ritzer, George, and Nathan Jurgenson (2010), "Production, Consumption, Prosumption: The Nature of Capitalism in the Age of the Digital 'Prosumer,'" *Journal of Consumer Culture*, 10, 1, 13–36.

Roy, Abhijit, and Satya P. Chattopadhyay (2010). "Stealth Marketing as a Strategy," *Business Horizons*, 53, 1, 69–79.

Saucet, Marcel (2004) "Le diamant: une veille stratégique sensorielle," Colloque de la veille stratégique, scientifique et technologique, Université Toulouse 3, 26 October.

Saucet, Marcel (2009), *Innovator: Innover face à la crise* [Innovator: innovation in the face of crisis], Nice, France: Éditions La Tour des Vents.

Saucet, Marcel, and Savario Tomasella (2006), "La marque consommée" [The brand consumed], 5èmes Journées normandes de recherche sur la consommation, Sociétés et Consommations, IAE de Caen, 23 et 24 mars.

Sawhney, Mohanbir, Gianmario Verona, and Emanuela Prandelli (2005), "Collaborating to Create: The Internet as a Platform for Customer Engagement in Product Innovation," *Journal of Interactive Marketing*, 19, 4, 4–17.

Shani, David, and Dennis M. Sandler (1998), "Ambush Marketing: Is Confusion to Blame for the Flickering or the Flame?" *Psychology & Marketing*, 15: 367–383.

Sharma, Subodh K. (2010), "Reviewing NGOs' Media Strategies: Possibilities for NGO–Media Collaboration," *Human and Natural Resources Studies*, Kathmandu University, Nepal.

Sherry Jr., John F., Robert V. Kozinets, and Stefania Borghini (2007), "Agents in Paradise: Experiential Co-Creation through Emplacement, Ritualization, and Community," in Carù, A., and Cova, B. (éds.), *Consuming Experiences*, London: Routledge, 2007, 17–33.

Tellis, Winston (1997), "Application of a Case Study Methodology," *The Qualitative Report*, 3, 3, September.

Uncles, Mark D. (2008), "Know Thy Changing Consumer," *Journal of Brand Management*, 15, 4, 227–231.

Vargo, Stephen L., and Robert F. Lusch (2004), "Evolving to a New Dominant Logic for Marketing," *Journal of Marketing*, 68, 1, 1–18.

Visconti, Luca M., John F. Sherry Jr., Stefania Borghini, and Laurel Anderson (2010), "Street Art, Sweet Art: The Reclamation of Public Place," *Journal of Consumer Research*, 37, 3, 511–529.

Von Hippel, Eric (1986), "Lead Users: A Source of Novel Product Concepts," *Management Science*, 32, 791–805.

Von Hippel, Eric (2005), *Democratizing Innovation*, Cambridge, MA: MIT Press.

West, Douglas, and John Ford (2001), "Advertising Agency Philosophies and Employee Risk Taking," *Journal of Advertising* 30, 1, 77–91.

Wipperfürth, Alex (2005), *Brand Hijack: Marketing without Marketing.* New York: Portfolio.

Index

About the Author

MARCEL SAUCET, PhD, is Professor Researcher at IPAG Business School in Paris, Research Associate at the University of San Diego, California, and co-writes case studies for the Harvard Business School. Saucet is the owner of the advertising agency Street Marketing™ by www.streetmarketing. buzz, a firm that specializes in guerrilla marketing in the street and innovation marketing. He holds street marketing conferences all around the world and lectures at business schools such as those at the University of Southern California, the University of Johannesburg, and BIMTech Institute of Delhi.